Foreword and In

This book is intended to give a general overview of the Chesapeake & Ohio Railway's operations in the state of West Virginia, mainly through high quality photos taken in the era from World War II up to the early 1960s.

This author wrote an 84 page book published by Carstens Publications in 1988 called *Mainlines & Mine Runs, The C&O in West Virginia*. Subsequent to that the C&O Historical Society published (1985) a detailed history of the Alleghany Subdivision, running from Clifton Forge, Va. to Hinton, W. Va. In 1989 the Society again released a book on C&O lines in the Mountain State entitled *Riding That New River Train*, which dealt with the C&O's New River Subdivision from Hinton, W. Va. to Handley, W. Va. with some data on the branches. William E. Sparkmon authored a book titled *The Chesapeake & Ohio Railway in West Virginia - Huntington Division* that dealt with the operations of the Kanawha Subdivision and some of its branches between Handley W. Va. and Huntington, W. Va. Additionally, the C&O Historical Society published (1995) a book entitled *Chesapeake & Ohio in the Coal Fields*, with a great deal of detail and many photos of the coal branches. But as of this writing (2005) all of these books are out of print. Furthermore they were intended for a market composed mainly of modelers and rail historians intensely interested in facts and details, and they covered the subject in considerable depth.

The intent of this work is not to replace these books, but supplement them by giving the general reader a less-detailed overview of the background and a history of C&O operations in West Virginia, using photos and extended captions. It is hoped that this will make the book desirable not only for the general reader, but also for the modeler and railfan interested in this region and this particular railway as a supplement to the visual presentations available in the other books mentioned.

People interested in the C&O tend to concentrate on this particular part of the system because it has great appeal to the modeler or historian. A number of factors are involved: First, it is in mountainous territory; second, it involves large trains of coal on the main lines and smaller mine runs on many branches woven among the mountains and valleys, dotted with mines. It has the added attraction of numerous coal towns and smaller cities and villages, large engine terminals and yards for assembling and forwarding trains, and a good volume of through overhead merchandise freight and numerous passenger trains. Lumbering and farming add more diversity.

Because of the terrain and service required, C&O used some of the largest and most powerful steam locomotives of all time in this area, and when diesels came C&O used a variety of early types in many different areas.

Like gold and silver mining in the West, coal mining in the East has its own nostalgia and broad interest. C&O in the period following World War II up to its merger with the Baltimore & Ohio (another line with much coal hauling in West Virginia, to the north of the C&O), was a well run, aggressive, well maintained, well financed, visionary company, run by some of the best people in railroading. They used the tremendous wealth generated from coal delivery to make the moderately sized C&O a powerhouse among railroads. This has led down to the present day. C&O financing allowed it to absorb B&O and Western Maryland, become Chessie System, and then consolidated with Seaboard System to become CSX Transportation, one of the four leading railroad systems left in the United States at this writing. I hope that the presentation of these photos will give a new appreciation for the C&O's many faces in West Virginia.

The treatment will start at Alleghany, Virginia, where C&O's main line crosses into West Virginia, and will end as it crosses over the Big Sandy River into northern Kentucky, it also includes the many branches radiating from the main line in this territory. Thanks are due to those who supplied photos, as indicated in the captions, to Bob DeVaul who did scans, and to Mac Beard who did the pre-press work.

Thomas W. Dixon, Jr.
Lynchburg, Va. January 2005.

Background - Origin and Development of the Chesapeake & Ohio Railway

The Chesapeake & Ohio Railway of the mid-late 20thCentury began its life over a century before as the tiny Louisa Railroad in Louisa County, Virginia, carrying farm products to market. In the era before the War Between The States it had changed its name to Virginia Central and had become an important element in Virginia railroading as the railway age in America developed. By 1856 it had reached the foot of the Appalachian Mountain range, and was poised, with the state's help, to build westward to the Ohio River. However, the war intervened, halting construction and crippling the existing lines since they were in many of the most contested battle areas.

After the war, northern capitalists led by Collis P. Huntington (who was just completing his work on the Central Pacific portion of the Transcontinental Railroad) took control and renamed the line "Chesapeake & Ohio" in keeping with its mission, and built it across the new state of West Virginia to the Ohio River. From that point Huntington eventually connected it with other lines he owned to form a true transcontinental for a few years, but lost control in 1889 to Vanderbilt interests. Under new President Melville Ingalls, C&O was rehabilitated, upgraded and rebuilt to the best standards and extended its line along the Ohio River to Cincinnati, enlarging its connections. C&O also gained trackage rights on what was later the Southern Railway to Washington, D. C. and arranged through traffic to New York via the Pennsylvania Railroad. Coal assumed its position as the most important commodity C&O was hauling as the great coal reaches of southern West Virginia were opened. Branch lines began to tap more coal areas, and C&O was launched on its successful era as a coal hauler.

From about 1900 through the early 1920s the coal market expanded and C&O built dozens of additional branches, not only in West Virginia but in the rich eastern Kentucky coal fields. In 1910 it gained financial control of the Hocking Valley Railway of Ohio and thus an easy outlet for its coal to the Great Lakes shipping. It also purchased the Chicago, Cincinnati, & Louisville Rail Road which operated between Cincinnati and Chicago. In the east C&O's lines had been completed to Newport News, Virginia, on the great Hampton Roads port opposite Norfolk, and the shipment was begun of coal to this point both for coastwise shipping by barge and ship to the northeast and all over the world.

C&O expanded its passenger service in 1889 with new through trains running from New York via Washington to Cincinnati and with through car connections to Chicago and Indianapolis.

By the early 1920s C&O was recognized as one of the most important coal haulers in the east, and control was acquired by the Van Sweringen brothers of Cleveland, who wove it into the tapestry of railroads under their control, including the Nickel Plate Road, the Erie, the Pere Marquette, and others. Through the 1920s C&O's business expanded and the line was upgraded and improved in all aspects from roadway to locomotives and cars.

During the Great Depression, when about 50% of American railroads were in bankruptcy, C&O was able to continue its program of improvements, building new tunnels, more second track, and generally improving all aspects of its line, because of its great cash reserves and the continued revenue from coal traffic. It merged the Hocking Valley's 300+ miles of line in Ohio into the C&O proper in 1930 and thus was set for a grand performance during World War II.

During the war C&O expanded coal hauling for war industries, carried all kinds of civilian goods and war material, and served the Hampton Roads Port of Embarkation for Europe.

Though well used by the end of the war the line was in great condition to capitalize on the postwar boom. Led by visionary Board Chairman Robert R. Young and highly competent, aggressive, forward looking executives and operating staff, C&O became a powerhouse in the mid-century as many other railroads began to suffer greatly from airline, highway, and barge competition.

Eventually, in the early 1960s, it took over Baltimore & Ohio and Western Maryland and integrated them into a highly competitive system even in the face of withering highway competition. It allied with another amalgam of well run Southeastern railroads in the form of Seaboard System and formed CSX Transportation in 1982. In the late 1990s CSX acquired parts of the old Northeastern railroad systems including a great deal of the old New York Central, and stands today as one of two major systems in the eastern U. S.

The Alleghany Subdivison

The story of the C&O in West Virginia as depicted in the following pages will unfold east-to-west following the main line and its branches describing and illustrating the railway's operations in this region using photos that represent the line at its apogee in the late steam and early diesel locomotive eras.

The mainline of the C&O arrives at the large terminal at Clifton Forge, Va. in two forks, one coming from Richmond through Lynchburg, following the James River, and the other coming from Richmond (joining the Washington line near Charlottesville), and over the rugged mountains and great Shenandoah Valley. At Clifton Forge they join for the trek west. Clifton Forge terminal was established by C&O in the late 1880s as the logical staging point to change locomotives and service cars and locomotives as they transitioned from one terrain to the other.

As the main line moves west from Clifton Forge it passes through the small city of Covington, and then begins the ascent of Alleghany Mountain. Once it reaches the summit, it crosses into West Virginia, and travels slightly down grade following the courses of several rivers on the Appalachian Plateau. The station at Alleghany, Virginia, was an important place for C&O mainline operations because, as the summit, it was the spot where trains could be relieved of pusher or helper locomotives, brakes tested, etc. It was a beehive of activity in the era with which we will deal, and a fitting gateway into the mountainous West Virginia. Note that in the Virginias Alleghany is spelled with an "a," not an "e".

Leaving the summit marker (2,080 feet) just west of Alleghany station, the C&O passes through Alleghany Tunnel, which actually crosses under the top of the ridge that forms the dividing line between Virginia and West Virginia, emerging on the western side at a site called Tuckahoe, W. Va. From that point it continues on a gentle grade westward for about five miles, reaching White Sulphur Springs, one of the "Springs of Virginia" so famous in the ante-bellum South and haven of city dwellers from the late 19th century forward. The Greenbrier Hotel, located at White Sulphur was built after the C&O itself acquired the property in 1910. Passenger traffic to and from this great resort was very important, and was still very strong in the era 1945-1960. From White Sulphur Springs the line continues about five miles into the Greenbrier River valley, joining that river at Whitcomb station, where the Greenbrier Branch of the C&O joined the main line. This branch was built right after the turn of the 20th Century to bring huge quantities of lumber and pulp wood from the vast forests of Greenbrier and Pocahontas Counties, and was important in this trade into the late 1950s.

A few miles west of Whitcomb is the small yard and terminal at Ronceverte, which always served as the terminal point for the Greenbrier Branch, with a small engine house and other facilities, and a uniquely designed station erected in 1915.

The line then follows the flow of the Greenbrier westward through Alderson, a small farming community, and other small rural stations. It then crosses under a spur of Big Bend Mountain through a tunnel made famous in song and literature by John Henry's epochal contest with the steam drill in the 1870s and finally arrives at the confluence of the Greenbrier and the New Rivers, where the division point and yard/shop was established at the town of Hinton. It was the western counterpart of Clifton Forge, serving as a transition from heavy grades to lighter ones as the line followed the New River west.

The line between Clifton Forge, Va. and Hinton, W. Va. was C&O's Alleghany Subdivision. In the era of discussion this line had little local traffic, the major industry being the large paper mill at Covington, Va., and the wood products originated on the Greenbrier branch. Otherwise the heavy traffic flowing over its double track was coal originating to the west headed for the coast, through fast freights, and passenger trains. A local freight working each direction took care of local business, switching and less than carload freight delivery.

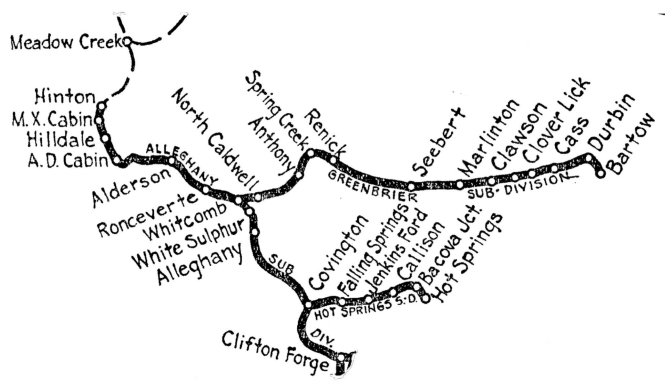

Map showing Alleghany Subdivision from Clifton Forge, Va. to Hinton, W. Va. About 47 miles of the 78-mile-long line is in West Virginia. Map from C&O employee timetable.

Alleghany, Va. was the station at the top of the mountain which forms the state border. At this point C&O maintained facilities for turning pusher locomotives. In this photo H-8 2-6-6-6 Allegheny type No. 1624 has just cut off after pushing from Hinton, W. Va. and is passing the altitude sign. It will return to Hinton light ready to push another train. The date is 1948. (NOTE: The locomotive is Allegheny with an "e" even though it is pictured at Alleghany with an "a".) *Gene Huddleston, COHS collection.*

(ABOVE) Allegheny type H-8 2-6-6-6 No. 1601 is being turned on the 115-ft. Alleghany, Va. turntable before its return to Hinton after pushing a coal train eastward over the mountain grade. The huge locomotive barely fit on the turntable. This September 1950 scene would be repeated only a couple more years before diesels made the locomotive and the turning operation obsolete.
Gene Huddleston, COHS collection.

(LEFT) Another of C&O's 60 Allegheny type H-8s is seen here westbound with mixed freight passing A Cabin at Alleghany. In a few hundred feet it will enter Alleghany Tunnel and while in the tunnel pass into West Virginia. The operator here (seen waving from the bay window) was a busy man, controlling switches for eastbound and westbound trains, and arranging to turn pushers and clear them back to Hinton.
B.F. Cutler, COHS collection.

(ABOVE) The portals of Alleghany Tunnel on the Virginia side, The first station on the C&O mainline in W. Va. is on the far side of these bores. *Bruce Fales, Jay Williams collection.*

(BELOW) This wonderful wide angle view shows an H-8 Allegheny with a typical eastbound coal train of the WWII era in the big curve at the top of the Alleghany grade at Tuckahoe, W. Va. The train will soon enter Alleghany Tunnel on its way toward the yard at Clifton Forge, Va. where coal will be made up in trains for the Newport News, Va. port. Today this area is grown up with trees and this photo can't be taken. *C&O Railway Photo, COHS collection.*

(Above) A C&O K-2 class 2-8-2 Mikado , No. 1203, has in tow a local freight working up the grade at Tuckahoe just before entering Alleghany Tunnel eastbound on May 9, 1951. Local freights carried a caboose on the front and rear of the train so as to provide space for brakemen making frequent switching moves as the train traversed the division dropping and picking up cars from freight stations, team tracks, and local industries. The K-2 came to the C&O in 1924 and at this late date was still a workhorse of the line. The type was fairly rare on the Alleghany Subdivision because of the need for big power for the very heavy coal trains, but in local freight work it was perfectly suited. *John Krause, COHS collection.*

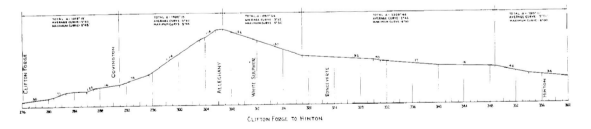

This profile shows how the Alleghany Subdivision laid on the geography of the area. From east-to-west it rose sharply from Covington to Alleghany. From west-to-east it rose gradually from Hinton to Alleghany. Because of the long, reasonably low gradient of 0.56% (about half a foot of rise for every 100 feet of track) it provided one of the easiest crossings of the Appalachian range, but still because of the heavy coal trains C&O wanted to move east, very large motive power was required, and pushers were needed.

C&O Manifest (fast freight) No. 98 is seen here eastbound with H-8 No.1619 in charge as it ascends the Alleghany grade eastward between White Sulphur Springs and Tuckahoe, W. Va. in June 1951. From the time of their arrival on the C&O beginning in 1941, the H-8s were standard power for all coal trains and fast freights between Hinton, W. Va. and Clifton Forge, Va. over the Alleghany grade. *Gene Huddleston, C&O Historical Society Collection.*

H-8 No. 1640 moves away from the camera as it climbs the grade along Dry Creek between White Sulphur Springs and Tuckahoe. Its clear exhaust and cloud of sand under the drivers indicate the amount of work it's doing on this, the steepest part of the Alleghany climb. This angle gives a good perspective on the size of the huge tender which dwarfs the trailing coal hopper car. The H-8s were the most powerful steam locomotive ever built when measured by horsepower. *Gene Huddleston, C&O Historical Society Collection.*

(ABOVE) With dieselization, C&O's passenger trains gave up their big steam power for EMD E8 passenger locomotives, such as No. 4022 seen here on Train No. 4, the eastbound *Sportsman* making a foggy morning call at the
trim white neo-Colonial station at White Sulphur Springs, W. Va. in the spring of 1955. Note the several tracks
behind the station which were used to park Pullman sleepers brought in for people visiting the Greenbrier resort
hotel, owned by C&O.

(BELOW) C&O Business Car "Chessie 29" is on one of the White Sulphur park tracks, while a string of sleepers is
on the track just behind the station, probably having come in on a special train.

(BOTH) C&O Railway photos, COHS collection.

Class K-3 2-8-2 Mikado No. 1251 with a local freight is switching cars at White Sulphur Springs in July 1947. Note the variety of older box cars being used for this. *J.I. Kelly, COHS collection.*

This 1958 photo shows GP9 No. 6233 leading four other similar units eastward with a coal train at White Sulphur Springs in September 1958. The five-unit diesel replaced an H-8 road engine and an H-8 pusher that would have handled this train up until about 1952.
Gene Huddleston, COHS collection.

Ronceverte's large brick station was unique in style on the C&O, with its upper floor containing offices. The building in the distance connected to the platform shed was the express and baggage area. The station still stands today.

C&O Railway photo. COHS collection

Just opposite the Ronceverte station was a small enginehouse and terminal accommodating locomotives in use on the Greenbrier branch, which ran 101 miles through Greenbrier and Pocahontas counties. This branch served numerous saw mills and carried wood products of all kinds. Seen here in 1949 is one of C&O Gas-Electric motor cars and a trailing combine car, used as the daily passenger train on the Greenbrier line. In the background is H-4 2-6-6-2 No. 1359. *T L. Wise photo. COHS collection.*

In this photo one of C&O's Gas-Electric motor trains has reached its terminal at Durbin, W. Va. near the end of the Greenbrier branch, about 1946. At this point the line joined with a Western Maryland line from Elkins. The Greenbrier branch was built in 1900 - 1903 to carry huge amounts of lumber and pulp wood from the giant mill at Cass, W. Va. and other locations, and declined after the forests began to be depleted. The Gas-Electric motor trains made their daily accommodation runs up the branch from Ronceverte until 1957. *John Karuse, COHS collection.*

No. 2760, one of C&O's all-purpose K-4 2-8-4 locomotives is at Renick, W. Va. on the Greenbrier line in 1953. The Greenbrier Subdivision was abandoned in 1978 and became a nature trail which hikers enjoy today. A small tourist railroad operates a few miles of the line out of Durbin.

Back on the main line K-3 No. 1229 roars out of Fort Spring Tunnel with a local freight westbound in 1947. The tunnel with its distinctive Art Deco portals was completed in June 1947 (note one track is still not ballasted) and allowed a long curve to be eliminated.

A late 1950s photo finds GP9 diesels exiting Fort Spring Tunnel. During the era from dieselization beginning in 1952 until the arrival of second generation diesels in the late 1960s, GP7s and GP9s were standard for almost all freight trains on this line. *(BOTH) C&O Railway photos, COHS collection.*

AD Cabin just west of Alderson, W. Va. station on the main line was typical of the many towers that dotted the line before the installation of Centralized Traffic Control. The tower accommodated an operator who copied train orders from the dispatcher, handed them up to trains, and controlled nearby switches. These towers were eliminated in the early 1960s.
W.R. Ford, COHS collection.

Pushers were used on all coal trains leaving Hinton, W. Va. and pushed all the way to Alleghany, Va., a distance of 48 miles. Here H-8 No. 1608 is working hard to help get the train to speed just east of Hinton yard in September 1947. Trains were generally up to 20-30 mph passing AD Cabin, but on the heaviest grade out of Ronceverte, they slowed to a crawl. *Charles H. Kerrigan*

(ABOVE) C&O Class H-7 2-8-8-2 No. 1560 powers an empty coal train west at Talcott, W. Va. in June 1943. Before the arrival of the H-8s, the H-7s had ruled the Alleghany line from their arrival in 1923-24. By the middle of WW II they had been entirely supplanted by H-8s. *C&O Railway photo, COHS collection.*

(ABOVE) The new Big Bend Tunnel at Talcott. The old tunnel continued to be used, with the new bore accommodating a second track. The tunnel is the site of the John Henry legend, when an African-American driller was supposely to have beaten the new Burleigh Steam Drill in a last stand of man against machine in the 1870s. (Highway historical marker at right.)

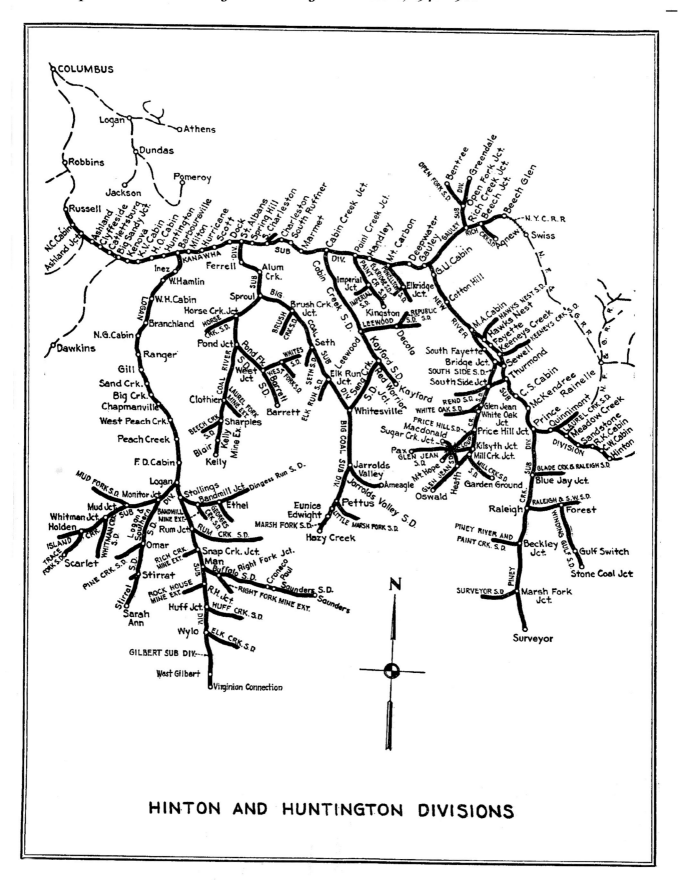

HINTON AND HUNTINGTON DIVISIONS

This map shows the bulk of the C&O in West Virginia, including the main line and all the branches west of Hinton. Combined with the map on page 4, one can see all of the C&O in West Virginia. As the map amply shows, C&O branches were built to tap many of the rich coal seams south of the main line. Taken from C&O Employee timetable.

The New River Subdivision

C&O's main line New River Subdivision ran from Hinton to Handley, W. Va., about 75 miles in length, following the New River through a rugged and beautiful gorge. From the main line numerous branches followed creeks and rivers north and south and tapped the rich underlying coal seams, funneling traffic to the main line. Once assembled in trains this prodigious flow of coal was sent eastward to the sea at Newport News, Va., and westward to the Great Lakes over C&O's Ohio and Indiana lines.

The C&O follows the New River out of Hinton along a fairly open valley for several miles. At Meadow Creek, 12 miles west of Hinton, the Nicholas, Fayette & Greenbrier Railroad joined the main line. This railroad was a coal hauler from the Greenbrier fields and was once important in logging the huge forest nearby through a massive mill at Rainelle. The NF&G was created in 1926 with some construction and consolidation of existing short lines and was jointly owned and operated by C&O and New York Central, connecting with NYC's old Kanawha & Michigan lines at Swiss, W. Va. The original line used several switchbacks to climb out of the New River valley, but these were replaced by broad loops in 1947. NF&G was an important contributor of traffic to C&O.

West of Meadow Creek the New River gorge crowds the C&O onto a narrow shelf for the next 46 miles to Gauley. This was a rugged, remote, and almost unsettled area until C&O arrived in the 1870s and through great effort carved out a line of railroad. Coal was found along the river and it began to be mined in the early 1880s. As coal was located in greater quantities further away from the main line, branches were constructed. At Quinnimont, 11 west of Meadow Creek, C&O had a small yard and engine terminal and served an iron furnace established here in the 1870s. Quinnimont later served as terminal for the Laurel Creek branch as well as the Piney Creek Branch, and was marshalling yard for large quantities of coal. The Piney Creek Branch reached Beckley, an important coal center, and radiated from its terminal at nearby Raleigh to numerous coal branches.

Only a mile west of Quinnimont was the station at Prince, near where the main line plunges through Stretcher's Neck Tunnel. Though a town of only a few dozen residents the station here was important for passenger traffic to and from Beckley, and in 1946 C&O built its most modern station building here in high Art Deco style. Ten miles beyond Prince is Thurmond, again a tiny town in population but one that always loomed large in C&O's operations as the hub of another huge coal mining region. From it, branches reached into the fields around Beckley as well, and to other areas. The yard and engine terminal were crowded along the river's edge. Because of it's wild boom-town reputation Thurmond is still remembered in local lore as well as for its railroad connection. At one time Thurmond produced more revenue for C&O than any other station. Its large two-story station and office building is now preserved and restored by the National Park Service as part of its New River Gorge National River operations and attracts much tourist attention.

Seven miles west of Thurmond was the town of Sewell, terminal for the narrow guage Mann's Creek Railroad that was in operation into the 1950s. At Sewell the C&O main line split, with one track hugging the north bank of the river and one crossing over to the south side. They joined again ten miles west at Macdougal, near Hawks Nest, where the line on the north side crossed over to the south. Hawks Nest was the junction of a short branch to a mine at Ansted, and site of a large hydroelectric dam erected in the 1930s. A State Park was established on US Route 60 running along the north rim of the gorge, with a scenic overlook. Here tourists could and still can look down on the C&O main line far below in the gorge.

C&O passes stations at Cotton Hill and Gauley where it emerges from the steepest portion of the gorge. Here the New and Gauley rivers join to form the Kanawha. The C&O line reaches the town of Montgomery, and a few miles west the division point at Handley, where the New River Subdivision ends and the Kanawha Subdivision begins.

(LEFT) H-8 No.1602 is seen here leaving Hinton's Avis Yard pushing an eastbound coal train in the summer of 1953, at the very end of steam, east of Hinton. The Greenbrier River is seen to the right. *Gene Huddleston, COHS collection.*

(BELOW) F-19 Pacific (4-6-2) No. 491 is on the point of local passenger train No. 8 stopped at the Hinton depot in June 1947. Pacific types were standard power for shorter passenger trains west of Hinton. No. 8 originated at Cincinnati and terminated here. *Gene Huddleston, COHS collection.*

HINTON YARD

HINTON LIES IN A MOUNTAINOUS AREA OF SOUTHERN WEST VIRGINIA AT A POINT WHERE THE GREENBRIAR RIVER FLOWS INTO THE NEW RIVER. ONLY SIX FAMILIES LIVED IN THE AREA WHEN THE RAILROAD ARRIVED. BOUGHT THE C&O DONATED THE LAND FOR THE PRESENT LAND, SUBDIVIDED IT, AND LAID OUT THE TOWN IN 1871. COURTHOUSE IN 1875, AND THE FOLLOWING YEAR HINTON BECAME THE COUNTY SEAT OF SUMMERS COUNTY.

A BUILDING BOOM BEGAN SHORTLY AFTER THE TOWN WAS FOUNDED AND LASTED UP TO THE TURN OF THE CENTURY. EXTANT RAILROAD STRUCTURES BUILT DURING THIS PERIOD INCLUDE THE FREIGHT DEPOT (1892), PASSENGER STATION (REBUILT AFTER A FIRE IN 1912), AND THE Y.M.C.A. BUILDING (1911). ALSO DURING THIS TIME TWO OPERA HOUSES, SEVERAL BANKS AND HOTELS, AND A NUMBER OF COMMERCIAL STRUCTURES WERE CONSTRUCTED. BY 1907 THE POPULATION HAD GROWN TO ABOUT SIX THOUSAND, A SIZABLE NUMBER OF WHICH RELIED ON THE C&O FOR THEIR LIVELIHOOD.

HINTON WAS CHOSEN AS A MAJOR DIVISION POINT ON THE C&O IN 1872, ONE OF TWELVE ON THE C&O MAINLINE. ITS SIGNIFICANCE TO THE RAILROAD CANNOT BE OVERSTATED, BECAUSE IT WAS THE POINT OF TRANSITION BETWEEN THE MOUNTAINOUS ALLEGHANY SUBDIVISION TO THE EAST, AND THE RUGGED NEW RIVER SUBDIVISION TO THE WEST. THE NARROW STRIP THAT IS NOW HINTON WAS DEVELOPED FROM THE START AS A MAJOR MAIN LINE RAIL CENTER BECAUSE OF ITS STRATEGIC LOCATION.

AT ITS PEAK, HINTON HAD A 17-ENGINE ROUNDHOUSE, FREIGHT DEPOT, SERVICE FACILITIES, AND TWO ASS-

EMBLY YARDS FOR THE MOVEMENT OF FREIGHT. FROM THE 1920S TO THE 1950S ITS STEAM ENGINES PUSHED COAL TRAIN AS FAR EAST AS ALLEGHANY, VIRGINIA. THE TWILIGHT OF STEAM IN THE 1950S AND THE CORPORATE MERGERS OF THE 1970S AND 1980S HAVE GREATLY DIMINISHED HINTON'S SIGNIFICANCE TO THE RAILROAD. A RICH INDUSTRIAL LEGACY REMAINS AT THE HINTON YARD, AND EXTANT RAIL-ROAD CONSTRUCTIONS LIKE THE FREIGHT DEPOT, PASSENGER STATION, AND COALING STATION ARE CRITICAL ELEMENTS OF IT.

HINTON'S SECOND ASSEMBLY YARD, AVIS YARD, LOCATED WEST OF THE HINTON YARD, ALONG THE NEW RIVER UNDERWENT MAJOR CHANGES IN THE 1930'S WHEN ADDITIONAL TRACKS WERE LAID, AND FACILITIES FOR REPAIR WERE CONSTRUCTED. NONE OF THE PRESENT STRUCTURES PREDATE THE 1940'S

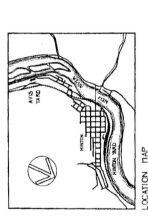

LOCATION MAP

No.	Structure	No.	Structure
27	SWITCHMEN'S SHANTY	64	ROUND HOUSE OFFICE
28	SIGNAL & WATER SUPPLY HOUSE	65	ROUND HOUSE
29	MOTOR CAR HOUSE	67	HOSTLER'S SHANTY
30	ICE HOUSE	68-1	BOILER SHOP
31	YARD SECTION LABORER'S HOUSE	68-2	BLACKSMITH SHOP
32	COAL DOCK FOR TOOL CARS	69	MACHINE SHOP
33	SCALE HOUSE	70	HOSE HOUSE
34	YARD MASTER'S OFFICE	71	OXY. ACETYLENE STORE ROOM
35	PUMP HOUSE	72	SHOP TOILET
36	ONE STORY FRAME HOUSE	73-1	OIL ROOM STORE HOUSE
37	HOSE HOUSE	73-2	OFFICE
38	MATERIAL RACK	74	BOILER WASHING PLANT
40	CAR REPAIR BLACKSMITHS SHOP	75	STORE ROOM
41	STORAGE AUTO TRUCK	76	WOODWORKING SHOP
42	PAINT HOUSE	77	PALLET ENGINE HOUSE
43	TOOL ROOM	78	STOKER MATERIAL
45	AIR ROOM	79	LUMBER SHED
46	ICE BOX	80	BATTERY CHARGING PLANT
47	OXYGEN ACETYLENE STORE HOUSE	81	OFFICE BUILDING
48	LUMBER SHED	82	BOILER HOUSE
49-1	OIL & DOPE HOUSE	83	COAL HOUSE
49-2	BOILER HOUSE	1A	PASSENGER STATION
50	WHEEL LATHE HOUSE	2A	RAILROAD Y.M.C.A.
51	YARD OFFICE	3A	FREIGHT HOUSE
52	RUNNING REPAIRMEN SHANTY	4A	STEEL WATER TANK
53	ENGINE INSPECTORS SHANTY	5A	WOOD WATER TANK
56	COAL BIN LABORER'S LOCKER HOUSE	6A	STEEL WATER TANK
58	APPRENTICE SCHOOL & OFFICE	7A	OIL TANKS
59	HOSE HOUSE	8A	OLD PUMP HOUSE
60	PIPE SHED	9A	ENGINE WASHING PLATFORM
61	PAINT SHED	10A	STOVE HOUSE
62	HOSE HOUSE	11A	COALING STATION
65	SHAVINGS HOUSE	12A	SAND HOUSE

EXTANT STRUCTURES ARE INDICATED IN A SOLID LINE, RETIRED STRUCTURES IN A DOTTED LINE.

C&O PROPERTY TAKEN FROM FIRE PREVENTION MAP, HINTON, VAL. SECT. V-11 DRAWING NO. 9240, JAN 1950, USING SAME CODES. ADDITIONAL STRUCTURES TAKEN FROM PLAN SHOWING 800 TON COALING STATION, HINTON, DRAWING NO. 9827, APRIL 1930

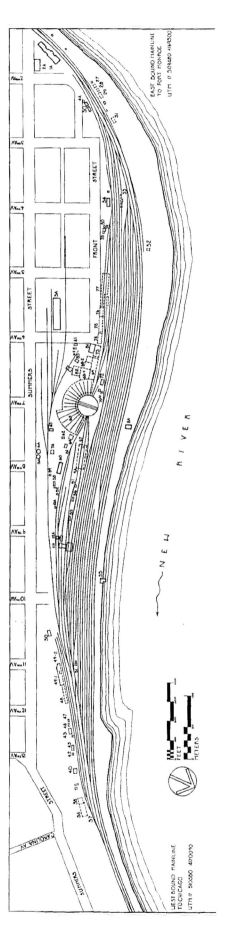

This map of Hinton showing all the principal terminal facilities was prepared by the Historic American Engineering Record in connection with a study they did to document structures at Thurmond and Hinton for the National Park Service, when the New River Gorge National River park was being established. It is an excellent summary of the Hinton yard and facilities, but doesn't include the Avis yard, which was east of the main part of the town. - (HAER Drawing No. WV-43 (Sheet 1) Delineated by Jennifer McCormick, 1988.)

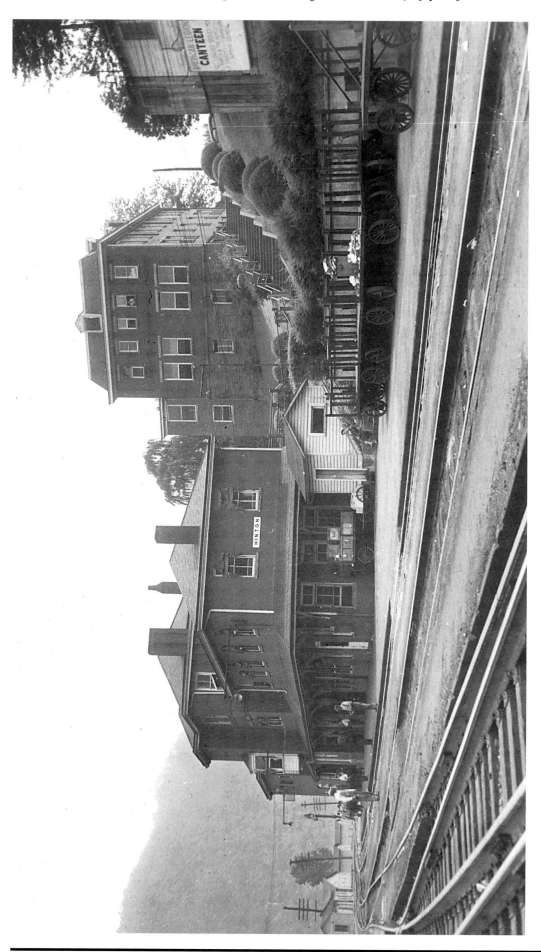

The large two-story red-brick Hinton depot was built in 1892, and added to several times over the years. The upper floors were used for division offices and dispatchers, while the ground floor accommodated waiting rooms, ticket office, baggage and express office and storage, as well as a lunchroom. The building on the hill just above the station was the Railroad YMCA where crews quartered during layovers. This 1947 scene shows the station area looking west. At this point the yard has narrowed to two mainlines and two additional tracks. The main yards are westward alongside the town and eastward at Avis. The building is still standing as of this writing with projects under way for restoration. *C&O Railway photo, COHS collection.*

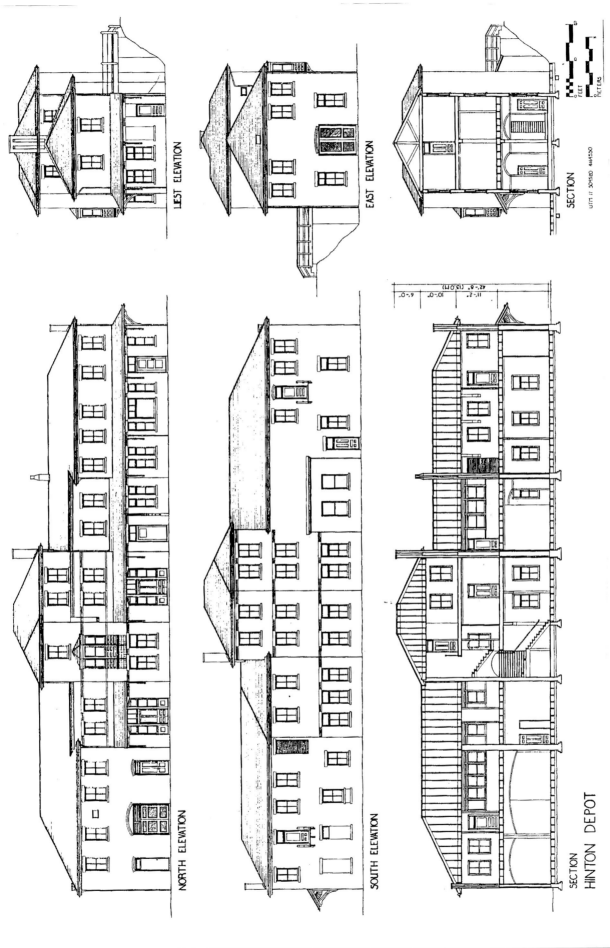

LEST ELEVATION

EAST ELEVATION

SECTION

NORTH ELEVATION

SOUTH ELEVATION

SECTION
HINTON DEPOT

This excellent drawing of the Hinton passenger station was prepared by the Historic American Engineering Record survey mentioned earlier, in 1988, and shows all four elevations as well as an interior cross section. Modelers will find that this is not reproduced to any particular scale, but can be scaled using the feet/meters legend in the lower right. (HAER Drawing WV-43A sheet 2).

This scene was typical when a train arrived at Hinton as passengers and crew waited to board. This shows Train 43 , the *Fast Flying Virginian's* second section, arriving in 1946. *(BOTH) Gene Huddleston, COHS collection.*

Hinton had two enginehouses: the roundhouse for smaller power, and the "Mallet House" shown here, for the big articulated locomotives, too large for the old roundhouse. Here, in 1947, H-8 No. 1621 sits ready to go eastward after having been serviced.

H-8 No.1625 is the centerpiece of this overhead view of the ready tracks near the coaling station at Hinton in 1947. The narrow yard and New River are in the background.
Gene Huddleston, COHS collection.

L-2 Hudson (4-6-4) No. 300 and H-8 1612 receive service at the Hinton ready tracks before taking runs westward. The big Hudson types were used for the heavy passenger trains westward out of Hinton. These trains were usually brought into Hinton from Charlottesville and Clifton Forge with Greenbrier (4-8-4) and Mountain (4-8-2) types.
C&O Railway photo, COHS collection.

C-16A 0-8-0 switcher No. 253 is seen here hard at work moving a cut of loaded coal cars through the Hinton yard in the winter of 1946. C&O's standard for switchers was the 0-8-0, though it employed giant 0-10-0s at Peach Creek Yard in the last 20 years of steam. The Hinton yard was jammed with cars in those days of heavy postwar freight movement. *(BOTH) C&O Railway photo, COHS collection.*

The operator has stepped out of his perch in the standard brick C&O signal tower at CW Cabin to hand up train orders for H-8 2-6-6-6 No.1614 as it leaves the Hinton yard westbound with a fast freight train (in curve in the distance). The red brick towers were a standard fixture over the C&O beginning in the 1920s.

(ABOVE) The first open station west of Hinton was Sandstone. Seen in 1956, the neat board-and-batten building dated from the first days of the C&O here in the 1870s and accommodated freight and passengers for the small settlement and it's surrounding countryside. The office's barred windows protected cash and valuables. Fire-barrels filled with sand and a bucket stand on the raised freight platform. A mail crane is seen in the left foreground for dispatch of mail to trains not stopping at this small station. (BELOW) A brace of 4 F7s, with No. 7080 leading, moves a train east past Sandstone Falls in New River in summer of 1956. *(BOTH) C&O Railway photo, COHS collection.*

(ABOVE) At Meadow Creek, only about three miles west of Sandstone, the Nicholas, Fayette & Greenbrier Railroad joined the C&O main line. This independently operated railroad was owned jointly by C&O and New York Central. C&O equipment was used on its part of the line. Here H-4 class 2-6-6-2s Nos. 1331 and 1419 rest in the small yard next to the main line.

(BELOW) To climb out of the New River valley NF&G used a series of switchbacks which were changed to sweeping loops in 1947. Here in 1952 a 2-6-6-2 brings empties up the loops at Claypool, W. Va. *(BOTH) B. J. Kern, COHS collection*

(ABOVE) H-4 No. 1411 with caboose 90665 behind pushes a train of empty hoppers on its way from the C&O main line to the NF&G terminal yard at Rainelle, W. Va. in 1952. The grade was so steep that even empty trains ascending it needed helpers.
B.J. Kern, COHS collection.

(LEFT) This map, taken from a employee timetable, shows the layout of the NF&G. The line had two major products, lumber and wood products from the giant Meadow River Lumber Company mill at Rainelle, and coal from many mines tapping the Greenbrier coal fields along its branches. Originated as a line connecting the lumber company to the C&O, it was acquired and consolidated jointly by C&O and NYC in the 1920s.

NICHOLAS. FAYETTE. & GREENBRIER RAILROAD

In 1952 two New York Central 2-8-2 Mikados shift with a C&O caboose at Rainelle Junction, in a truly joint operation. NYC's connection with NF&G was at Swiss, W. Va. (see map on previous page), where NYC's K&M line came in from Charleston and central Ohio. *B. J. Kern, COHS collection*

Rainelle's NF&G engine terminal was usually filled with C&O 2-6-6-2s when they weren't out on mine runs or taking trains up and down the loops to the C&O main at Meadow Creek. In July 1952 three of these powerful locomotives while a smaller NYC 2-8-2 rests at right and a string of C&O wooden cabooses sits in the background, another characteristic feature of the place. *B. J. Kern, COHS collection*

This photo shows transition between steam and diesel on NF&G as C&O GP7's Nos. 5813/5844 rest beside NYC 2-8-2 No. 6405 at the Rainelle engine house in September 1954. *COHS collection.*

This aerial view shows Meadow River Lumber Company's huge mill and yard of stacked lumber and the town of Rainelle about 1952. The NF&G terminal is in the upper left, with its line to the coal fields running off to the lower right. *COHS collection.*

(LEFT) About 12 miles west of Meadow Creek on the mainline and deep in the New River Gorge is the small terminal yard at Quinnimont, W. Va. where trains were assembled to and from the Laurel Creek branch and the Piney Creek Subdivision and its maze of coal branches. Taken in 1954 the station area is at left with worker's housing to the right. Four GP9s take empties east. The freight station and yard office (QN Cabin) are in the distance to the left.

C&O Railway photo,
COHS collection.

(BELOW) This map gives an idea of the Y-shaped yard and terminal at Quinnimont.

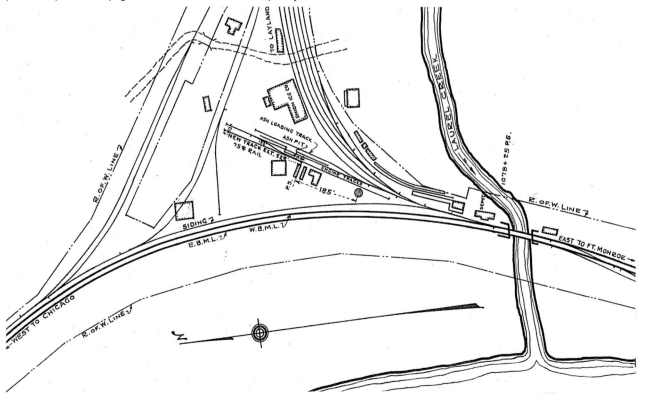

Here H-8 No. 1615 moves a coal train east through Quinnimont yard. To the right is the tall wooden water tank, long a landmark here, and to its left the boiler house that supplied steam for the water pump and heat throughout the facility. *Gene Huddleston, COHS collection.*

QN Cabin, serving as the yard office stood until the 1980s as the last combined tower/depot structures on the C&O. This night photo gives a real flavor for the place as it was, even in later days. *Ron Piskor*

(ABOVE) Less than a mile west of Quinnimont is Prince, were a Piney Creek branch leaves the main line and crosses New River (the bridge is in background) toward Beckley and the coal branches that radiate from there. This 1945 photo shows the wood frame station and NI Cabin tower at Prince just before the station was replaced by an Art Deco depot (below) that was the only one actually built of a number planned. It served not just the 50 or so people of Prince, but the large population of Beckley, a few miles up the mountain. Still in service for Amtrak, the large modernistic station looks completely out of place in its isolated environment. *(BOTH) C&O Railway photos, COHS collection.*

In 1946 the woman operator at NI Cabin prepares to hand up train orders to crew of C&O H-6 No. 1481 as it takes an empty hopper train up the Piney Creek Branch toward Raleigh Yard at Beckley, where the cars will be distributed to scores of mines radiating from that point.

(BOTH) C&O Railway photos, COHS collection.

Emblematic of C&O's West Virginia operations is this scene with doubleheaded H-6 2-6-6-2 Mallets, led by No.1479 bringing a heavy coal train down the Piney Creek Gorge to Quinnimont where the cars will be prepared for shipment east or west. From the 1920s to the end of steam in the mid-1950s C&O used its fleet of 2-6-6-2 compound articulated locomotives on mine runs of all kinds because of their high tractive power and short rigid wheel bases, which allowed moving heavy loads on curvy lines.

From Prince the Piney Creek Subdivision led up to a coal marshalling yard at Raleigh, near Beckley, a center of coal mining in the region. Here H-4 2-6-6-2 Mallet No. 1397 gets service while H-6 No.1489 simmers in the background near the coaling station. This scene was repeated many times a day as locomotives were readied to take empty cars to the mines and pull loads back here. They were assembled into trains and taken to Quinnimont for pickup by main line trains and transportation to Clifton Forge to be forwarded eastward or Russell to be sent westward.
C&O Railway photo, COHS collection.

One of the branches served by Raleigh was the Winding Gulf Subdivision, which served numerous mines jointly with the Virginian Railway, and crossed and recrossed that railway in the region. Here H-4 2-6-6-2s Nos. 1418 and 1412 run light after pushing a train at Gulf Switch, W.Va.

J.I.Kelly, COHS collection.

The Winding Gulf Coals, Inc. mine at MacAlpin, W. Va. was served by both Virginian and C&O as can be seen by the variety of hopper cars from both lines under the tipple in this June 1954 photo. With its corrugated steel sides the tipple here was quite typical of West Virginia mines of the era.

Another of Winding Gulf Coal Company's mines was at Tams, W. Va. The tipple here is of frame design with board-and-batten siding, another style that was often seen in this region of the coal fields. The C&O hoppers coming out from under the tipple have been loaded with fine coal probably for use in big boilers equipped with stokers. The tipple served to clean and grade coal, and separate impurities. *(BOTH) C&O Railway photo, COHS collection.*

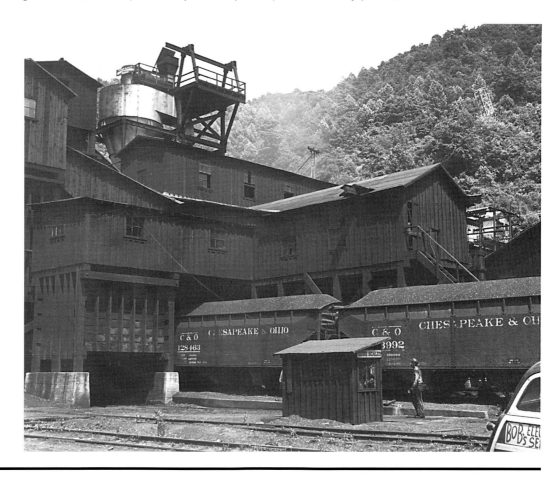

(TOP) New River Company's mine at Summerlee, W. Va. is seen here in 1954 with coal of differing sizes loaded in C&O hoppers. This mine has a hoist house for its shaft. (ALL) COHS collection.

(ABOVE) The Gulf Smokeless Coal Mine at Tams is seen here again from a different view with C&O H-4 No. 1445 and another locomotive with a caboose moving alongside the tipple. They must be here to pick up the loads seen at left.

(LEFT) Back on the main line, we see some maintenance work under way in 1945. These track men were typical of the large labor forces needed to keep the C&O's trackage up to standard because of the wear and tear on it by steam locomotives and heavy trains. It was a labor-intensive job with hand tools until the 1950s.

(ABOVE) In the summer of 1953 steam was still active in Thurmond, W. Va. Here G-9 2-8-0 No. 1041 runs light past the large Thurmond depot. Thurmond was one of the most interesting places in the C&O coal fields and has had much written about it. The station was once the largest revenue producer on the C&O because of all the coal billed out of its offices.

(ALL) Gene Huddleston, COHS collection

C&O G7's 2-8-0 Nos. 975 and 990 in Thurmond yard 1953

(LEFT) H-8 2-6-6-6 No. 1624 moves its train eastward after having taken on coal at the Thurmond coaling station September 1955.

NOTE. The C&O Historical Society produces a 48-page booklet on Thurmond as well as a Compact Disc with scores of additional photos and maps. Contact the Society at 800-453-COHS or www.chessieshop.com

The enginehouse at Thurmond was a long board-and-batten affair that could accommodate four large 2-6-6-2 types inside at once. G-7 and G-9 2-8-0s and H-4 and H-6 2-6-6-2s were the most common power at Thurmond in the period from the 1920s forward. After the coming of diesels they were replaced uniformly by GP7s and GP9s. *(Photo courtesy of D. Wallace Johnson)*

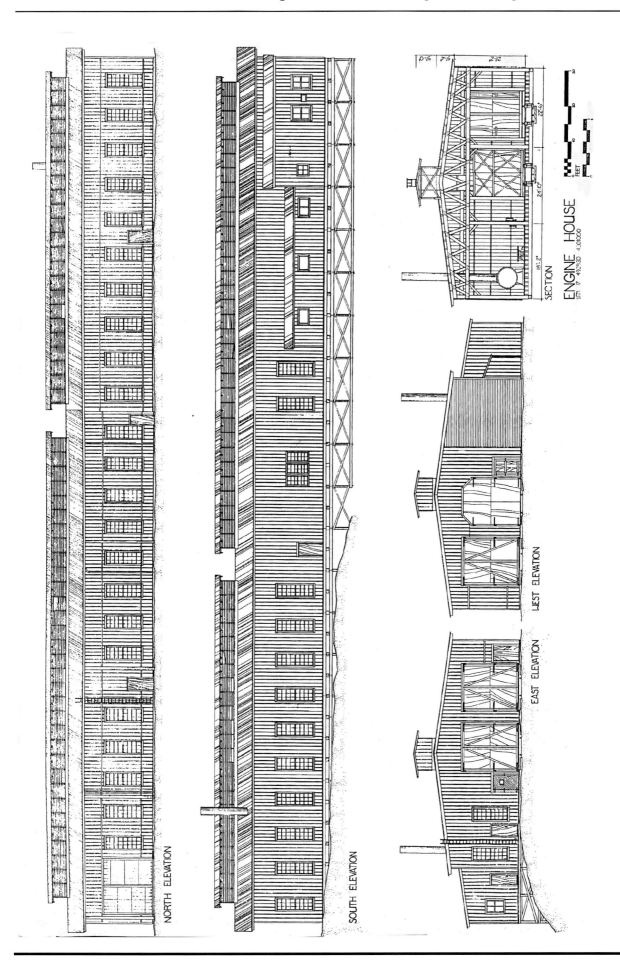

NORTH ELEVATION

SOUTH ELEVATION

EAST ELEVATION

WEST ELEVATION

ENGINE HOUSE

SECTION

This drawing of the Thurmond enginehouse was made by the Historic American Engineering Record during its documentation of the facilities here for the National Park Service. The drawing can be scaled by using the legend at right. (From HAER drawing No. WV-42B Sheet 2) NOTE: A complete set of full sized (24x36 inches) Thurmond HAER drawings is available from C&O Hist. Soc. at 800-453-COHS or www.chessieshop.com (under drawings).

(LEFT) The coke ovens for Royalty Smokeless Coal Company were in operation at Sewell, W. Va. after most other operations of a similar nature in the New River Gorge area had closed. This 1955 photo shows workers pulling coke from brick ovens right along the C&O main line and loading it into hoppers. At one time almost every mine along the gorge had banks of coke ovens and the smoke by day and glow of fire by night reminded train travelers of the fires of the underworld as they glided by on C&O's main line.

(BELOW) Typical of drift mines located along the sides of New River Gorge was Southern Coals Corp. Cunard No. 2 mine at Cunard, W. Va., seen here in 1954. The headhouse at the mine is far up the side where the coal seam lies. Coal is transported in pulley cars down to the tipple, over the C&O tracks, where the coal was graded and dumped into cars.

(BOTH) C&O Railway photos, COHS collection.

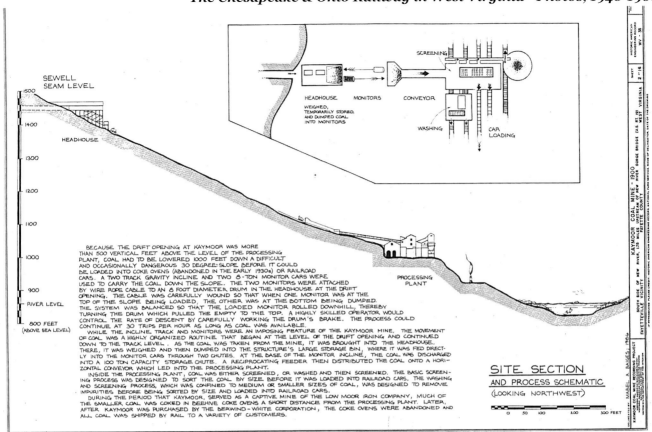

SEWELL
SEAM LEVEL

1500

1400

HEADHOUSE

1300

1200

1100

1000

RIVER LEVEL

900

800 FEET
(ABOVE SEA LEVEL)

SCREENING

HEADHOUSE   MONITORS   CONVEYOR

WEIGHED,
TEMPORARILY STORED,
AND DUMPED COAL
INTO MONITORS

WASHING   CAR
LOADING

PROCESSING
PLANT

BECAUSE THE DRIFT OPENING AT KAYMOOR WAS MORE THAN 500 VERTICAL FEET ABOVE THE LEVEL OF THE PROCESSING PLANT, COAL HAD TO BE LOWERED 1000 FEET DOWN A DIFFICULT AND OCCASIONALLY DANGEROUS 30 DEGREE SLOPE BEFORE IT COULD BE LOADED INTO COKE OVENS (ABANDONED IN THE EARLY 1930s) OR RAILROAD CARS. A TWO TRACK GRAVITY INCLINE AND TWO 8-TON MONITOR CARS WERE USED TO CARRY THE COAL DOWN THE SLOPE. THE TWO MONITORS WERE ATTACHED BY WIRE ROPE CABLE TO AN 8 FOOT DIAMETER DRUM IN THE HEADHOUSE AT THE DRIFT OPENING. THE CABLE WAS CAREFULLY WOUND SO THAT WHEN ONE MONITOR WAS AT THE TOP OF THE SLOPE BEING LOADED, THE OTHER WAS AT THE BOTTOM BEING DUMPED. THE SYSTEM WAS BALANCED SO THAT THE LOADED MONITOR ROLLED DOWNHILL, THEREBY TURNING THE DRUM WHICH PULLED THE EMPTY TO THE TOP. A HIGHLY SKILLED OPERATOR WOULD CONTROL THE RATE OF DESCENT BY CAREFULLY WORKING THE DRUM'S BRAKE. THE PROCESS COULD CONTINUE AT 30 TRIPS PER HOUR AS LONG AS COAL WAS AVAILABLE.

WHILE THE INCLINE, TRACK AND MONITORS WERE AN IMPOSING FEATURE OF THE KAYMOOR MINE, THE MOVEMENT OF COAL WAS A HIGHLY ORGANIZED ROUTINE THAT BEGAN AT THE LEVEL OF THE DRIFT OPENING AND CONTINUED DOWN TO THE TRACK LEVEL. AS THE COAL WAS TAKEN FROM THE MINE, IT WAS BROUGHT INTO THE HEADHOUSE. THERE, IT WAS WEIGHED AND THEN DUMPED INTO THE STRUCTURE'S LARGE STORAGE BIN, WHERE IT WAS FED DIRECTLY INTO THE MONITOR CARS THROUGH TWO CHUTES. AT THE BASE OF THE MONITOR INCLINE, THE COAL WAS DISCHARGED INTO A 100 TON CAPACITY STORAGE CHUTE. A RECIPROCATING FEEDER THEN DISTRIBUTED THE COAL ONTO A HORIZONTAL CONVEYOR WHICH LED INTO THE PROCESSING PLANT.

INSIDE THE PROCESSING PLANT, COAL WAS EITHER SCREENED, OR WASHED AND THEN SCREENED. THE BASIC SCREENING PROCESS WAS DESIGNED TO SORT THE COAL BY SIZE BEFORE IT WAS LOADED INTO RAILROAD CARS. THE WASHING AND SCREENING PROCESS, WHICH WAS CONFINED TO MEDIUM OR SMALLER SIZES OF COAL, WAS DESIGNED TO REMOVE IMPURITIES BEFORE BEING SORTED BY SIZE AND LOADED INTO RAILROAD CARS.

DURING THE PERIOD THAT KAYMOOR SERVED AS A CAPTIVE MINE OF THE LOW MOOR IRON COMPANY, MUCH OF THE SMALLER COAL WAS COKED IN BEEHIVE COKE OVENS A SHORT DISTANCE FROM THE PROCESSING PLANT. LATER, AFTER KAYMOOR WAS PURCHASED BY THE BERWIND-WHITE CORPORATION, THE COKE OVENS WERE ABANDONED AND ALL COAL WAS SHIPPED BY RAIL TO A VARIETY OF CUSTOMERS.

SITE SECTION
AND PROCESS SCHEMATIC
(LOOKING NORTHWEST)

0   50   100   200   300 FEET

These two HAER drawings show the headhouse and the "monitor" leading down to the tipple at track level for the Kaymoor mine which was only about eight miles from the Cunard operation pictured on the opposite page and very similar in configuration.

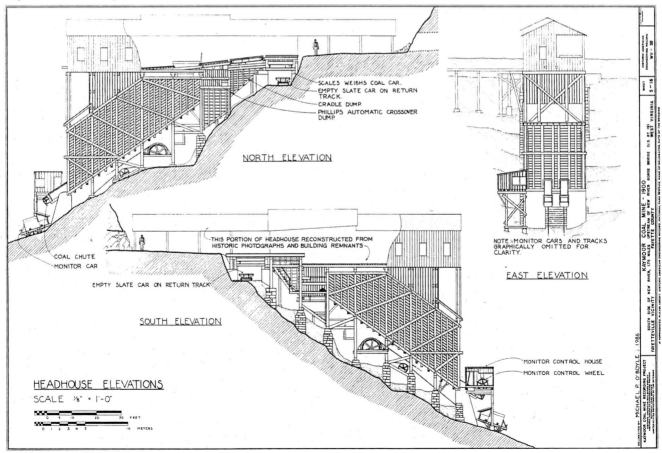

SCALES WEIGHS COAL CAR.
EMPTY SLATE CAR ON RETURN TRACK.
CRADLE DUMP.
PHILLIPS AUTOMATIC CROSSOVER DUMP.

NORTH ELEVATION

NOTE MONITOR CARS AND TRACKS GRAPHICALLY OMITTED FOR CLARITY.

EAST ELEVATION

THIS PORTION OF HEADHOUSE RECONSTRUCTED FROM HISTORIC PHOTOGRAPHS AND BUILDING REMNANTS

COAL CHUTE
MONITOR CAR

EMPTY SLATE CAR ON RETURN TRACK

SOUTH ELEVATION

MONITOR CONTROL HOUSE
MONITOR CONTROL WHEEL

HEADHOUSE ELEVATIONS
SCALE ⅛" = 1'-0"

0   5   10   20   30 FEET
0 1 2 3 4 5   10 METERS

This HAER drawing shows the tipple at Kaymoor mine. This mine and tipple are typical of mines located along the C&O in the New River area. If modelers want to use the drawing, ignore the 1/8-inch scale since the drawing has been reduced, and use the bar scale shown in the legend. (HAER drawing WV-38, sheet 10). (NOTE: A complete set of full sized (24x36) drawings of the Kaymoor mine showing all aspects of its operation is available from C&O Hist. Society 800-453-COHS or www.chessieshop.com (look under drawings).

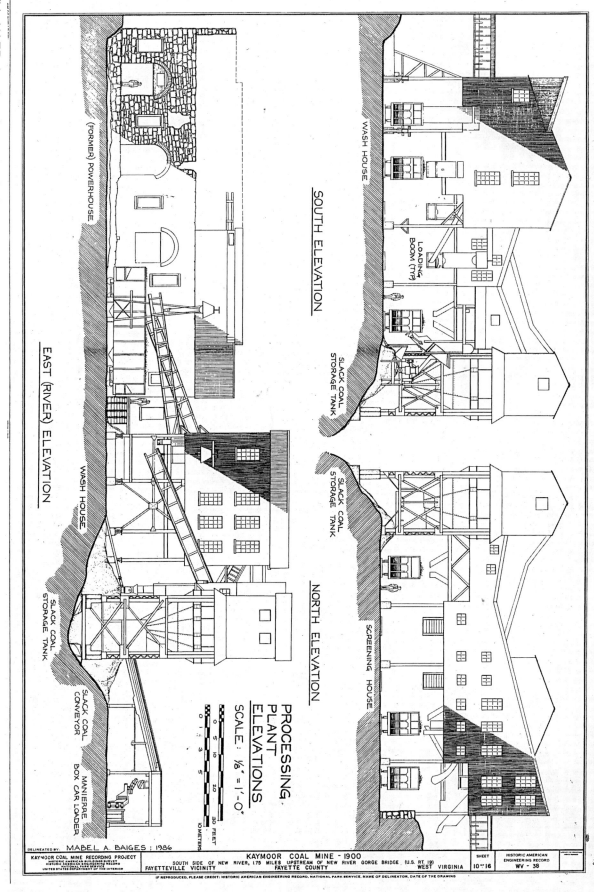

SOUTH ELEVATION

WASH HOUSE

LOADING BOOM (TYP)

SLACK COAL STORAGE TANK

(FORMER) POWERHOUSE

EAST (RIVER) ELEVATION

WASH HOUSE

SLACK COAL STORAGE TANK

SLACK COAL CONVEYOR

MANIERRE BOX CAR LOADER

NORTH ELEVATION

SLACK COAL STORAGE TANK

SCREENING HOUSE

PROCESSING PLANT ELEVATIONS

SCALE: 1/8" = 1'-0"

DELINEATED BY: MABEL A. BAIGES ; 1986

KAYMOOR COAL MINE RECORDING PROJECT
HISTORIC AMERICAN BUILDINGS SURVEY
HISTORIC AMERICAN ENGINEERING RECORD
NATIONAL PARK SERVICE
UNITED STATES DEPARTMENT OF THE INTERIOR

KAYMOOR COAL MINE - 1900
SOUTH SIDE OF NEW RIVER, 1.75 MILES UPSTREAM OF NEW RIVER GORGE BRIDGE (U.S. RT. 19)
FAYETTEVILLE VICINITY   FAYETTE COUNTY   WEST VIRGINIA

SHEET	HISTORIC AMERICAN ENGINEERING RECORD
10 OF 16	WV - 38

IF REPRODUCED, PLEASE CREDIT: HISTORIC AMERICAN ENGINEERING RECORD, NATIONAL PARK SERVICE, NAME OF DELINEATOR, DATE OF THE DRAWING

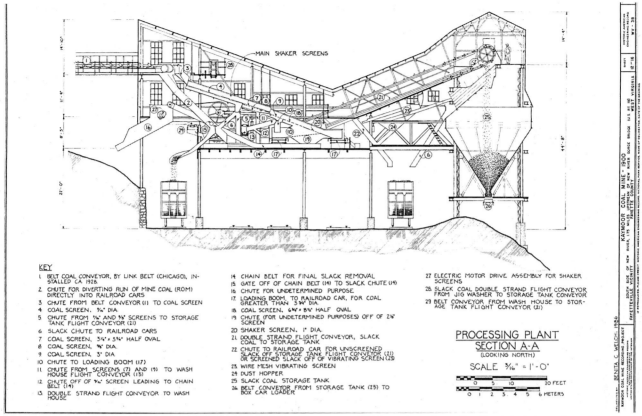

MAIN SHAKER SCREENS

KEY

1 BELT COAL CONVEYOR, BY LINK BELT (CHICAGO), IN-STALLED CA. 1928.
2 CHUTE FOR DIVERTING RUN OF MINE COAL (ROM) DIRECTLY INTO RAILROAD CARS
3 CHUTE FROM BELT CONVEYOR (1) TO COAL SCREEN
4 COAL SCREEN, 3/8" DIA.
5 CHUTE FROM 3/8" AND 5/8" SCREENS TO STORAGE TANK FLIGHT CONVEYOR (21)
6 SLACK CHUTE TO RAILROAD CARS
7 COAL SCREEN, 3 1/4" x 3 1/4" HALF OVAL
8 COAL SCREEN, 3/8" DIA.
9 COAL SCREEN, 3" DIA.
10 CHUTE TO LOADING BOOM (17)
11 CHUTE FROM SCREENS (7) AND (9) TO WASH HOUSE FLIGHT CONVEYOR (13)
12 CHUTE OFF OF 3/4" SCREEN LEADING TO CHAIN BELT (14)
13 DOUBLE STRAND FLIGHT CONVEYOR TO WASH HOUSE

14 CHAIN BELT FOR FINAL SLACK REMOVAL
15 GATE OFF OF CHAIN BELT (14) TO SLACK CHUTE (14)
16 CHUTE FOR UNDETERMINED PURPOSE
17 LOADING BOOM, TO RAILROAD CAR, FOR COAL GREATER THAN 3 3/4" DIA.
18 COAL SCREEN, 6 3/4" x 8 1/4" HALF OVAL
19 CHUTE (FOR UNDETERMINED PURPOSES) OFF OF 2 1/8" SCREEN
20 SHAKER SCREEN, 1" DIA.
21 DOUBLE STRAND FLIGHT CONVEYOR, SLACK COAL TO STORAGE TANK
22 CHUTE TO RAILROAD CAR FOR UNSCREENED SLACK OFF STORAGE TANK FLIGHT CONVEYOR (21) OR SCREENED SLACK OFF OF VIBRATING SCREEN (23)
23 WIRE MESH VIBRATING SCREEN
24 DUST HOPPER
25 SLACK COAL STORAGE TANK
26 BELT CONVEYOR FROM STORAGE TANK (25) TO BOX CAR LOADER

27 ELECTRIC MOTOR DRIVE ASSEMBLY FOR SHAKER SCREENS
28 SLACK COAL DOUBLE STRAND FLIGHT CONVEYOR FROM JIG WASHER TO STORAGE TANK CONVEYOR
29 BELT CONVEYOR FROM WASH HOUSE TO STOR-AGE TANK FLIGHT CONVEYOR (21)

PROCESSING PLANT SECTION A-A
(LOOKING NORTH)
SCALE 3/16" = 1'-0"

These drawings taken from the HAER study of the Kaymoor, W.Va. mine show the tipple's internal workings and the track layout at the tipple. - Those interested in mines should purchase the full sized drawings available as indicated on the previous page.

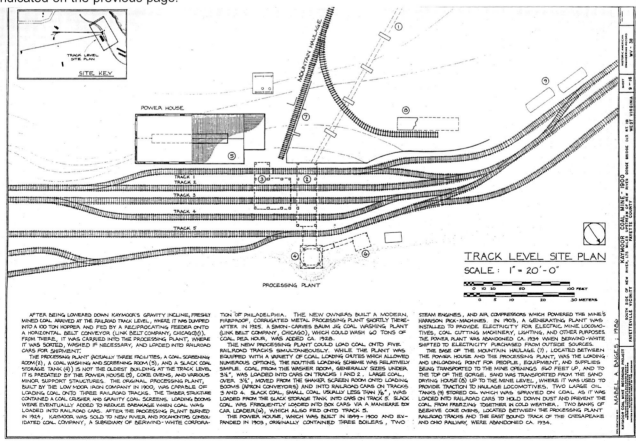

SITE KEY

TRACK LEVEL SITE PLAN

MOUNTAIN HAULAGE

POWER HOUSE

TRACK 1
TRACK 2
TRACK 3
TRACK 4
TRACK 5

PROCESSING PLANT

TRACK LEVEL SITE PLAN
SCALE : 1" = 20'-0"

AFTER BEING LOWERED DOWN KAYMOOR'S GRAVITY INCLINE, FRESHLY MINED COAL ARRIVED AT THE RAILROAD TRACK LEVEL, WHERE IT WAS DUMPED INTO A 100 TON HOPPER AND FED BY A RECIPROCATING FEEDER ONTO A HORIZONTAL BELT CONVEYOR (LINK BELT COMPANY, CHICAGO)(1). FROM THERE, IT WAS CARRIED INTO THE PROCESSING PLANT, WHERE IT WAS SORTED, WASHED IF NECESSARY, AND LOADED INTO RAILROAD CARS FOR SHIPMENT.

THE PROCESSING PLANT (ACTUALLY THREE FACILITIES, A COAL SCREENING ROOM (2), A COAL WASHING AND SCREENING ROOM (3), AND A SLACK COAL STORAGE TANK (4)) IS NOT THE OLDEST BUILDING AT THE TRACK LEVEL. IT IS PREDATED BY THE POWER HOUSE (5), COKE OVENS, AND VARIOUS MINOR SUPPORT STRUCTURES. THE ORIGINAL PROCESSING PLANT, BUILT BY THE LOW MOOR IRON COMPANY IN 1900, WAS CAPABLE OF LOADING COAL ONTO THREE RAILROAD TRACKS. THE TIMBER STRUCTURE CONTAINED A COAL CRUSHER AND GRAVITY COAL SCREENS. LOADING BOOMS WERE EVENTUALLY ADDED TO REDUCE BREAKAGE WHEN COAL WAS LOADED INTO RAILROAD CARS. AFTER THE PROCESSING PLANT BURNED IN 1924, KAYMOOR WAS SOLD TO NEW RIVER AND POCAHONTAS CONSOL-IDATED COAL COMPANY, A SUBSIDIARY OF BERWIND-WHITE CORPORA-

TION OF PHILADELPHIA. THE NEW OWNERS BUILT A MODERN, FIREPROOF, CORRUGATED METAL PROCESSING PLANT SHORTLY THERE-AFTER IN 1925. A SIMON-CARVES BAUM JIG COAL WASHING PLANT (LINK BELT COMPANY, CHICAGO), WHICH COULD WASH 60 TONS OF COAL PER HOUR, WAS ADDED CA. 1928.

THE NEW PROCESSING PLANT COULD LOAD COAL ONTO FIVE RAILROAD TRACKS SIMULTANEOUSLY. WHILE THE PLANT WAS EQUIPPED WITH A VARIETY OF COAL LOADING CHUTES WHICH ALLOWED NUMEROUS OPTIONS, THE ROUTINE LOADING SCHEME WAS RELATIVELY SIMPLE. COAL FROM THE WASHER ROOM, GENERALLY SIZES UNDER 3 1/4", WAS LOADED INTO CARS ON TRACKS 1 AND 2. LARGE COAL, OVER 3 1/4", MOVED FROM THE SHAKER SCREEN ROOM ONTO LOADING BOOMS (APRON CONVEYORS) AND INTO RAILROAD CARS ON TRACKS 3 AND 4. SLACK COAL, SMALL COAL USUALLY LESS THAN 1/8", WAS LOADED FROM THE SLACK STORAGE TANK INTO CARS ON TRACK 5. SLACK COAL WAS FREQUENTLY LOADED INTO BOX CARS VIA A MANIERRE BOX CAR LOADER (4), WHICH ALSO FED ONTO TRACK 5.

THE POWER HOUSE, WHICH WAS BUILT IN 1899-1900 AND EX-PANDED IN 1903, ORIGINALLY CONTAINED THREE BOILERS, TWO

STEAM ENGINES, AND AIR COMPRESSORS WHICH POWERED THE MINE'S HARRISON PICK-MACHINES. IN 1903, A GENERATING PLANT WAS INSTALLED TO PROVIDE ELECTRICITY FOR ELECTRIC MINE LOCOMO-TIVES, COAL CUTTING MACHINERY, LIGHTING, AND OTHER PURPOSES. THE POWER PLANT WAS ABANDONED CA. 1934 WHEN BERWIND-WHITE SHIFTED TO ELECTRICITY PURCHASED FROM OUTSIDE SOURCES.

THE BASE OF THE MOUNTAIN HAULAGE (7), LOCATED BETWEEN THE POWER HOUSE AND THE PROCESSING PLANT, WAS THE LOADING AND UNLOADING POINT FOR PEOPLE, EQUIPMENT, AND SUPPLIES BEING TRANSPORTED TO THE MINE OPENINGS 540 FEET UP, AND TO THE TOP OF THE GORGE. SAND WAS TRANSPORTED FROM THE SAND DRYING HOUSE (8) UP TO THE MINE LEVEL, WHERE IT WAS USED TO PROVIDE TRACTION TO HAULAGE LOCOMOTIVES. TWO LARGE OIL TANKS (9) STORED OIL WHICH WAS SPRAYED ON COAL AS IT WAS LOADED INTO RAILROAD CARS TO HOLD DOWN DUST AND PREVENT THE COAL FROM FREEZING TOGETHER IN COLD WEATHER. TWO BANKS OF BEEHIVE COKE OVENS, LOCATED BETWEEN THE PROCESSING PLANT RAILROAD TRACKS AND THE EAST BOUND TRACK OF THE CHESAPEAKE AND OHIO RAILWAY, WERE ABANDONED CA. 1934.

In the fall of 1947 C&O K-4 class 2-8-4 Kanawha type steam locomotive No. 2745 leads a westbound freight across the New River at Macdougal, W. Va. (opposite side of the river Hawks Nest station). Visitors to Hawks Nest State Park can look down on this scene today (minus the steam engine and building, of course!)

(BOTH) C&O Railway photos, COHS collection.

(ABOVE) A C&O Allegheny type takes a coal train along New River deep in the gorge in the summer of 1947.

F7 ABA set of road diesels led by 7004 pulls manifest freight Train No. 92 east at Blue Hole, W. Va. in the darkest part of the New River Gorge in 1956. The many tank cars are undoubtedly chemicals from Charleston. *Gene Huddleston, COHS collection.*

H-8 No. 1642 is seen here eastbound with a coal train passing Cotton Hill, W. Va. station, the rocky New River forming a dramatic background ca. 1948. This locomotive was later destroyed in a boiler explosion at Hinton, W. Va.

B.F. Cutler, COHS colection.

(BELOW) Three C&O E8's, No. 4011 in the lead, are in charge of Train No. 3, the westbound *Fast Flying Virginian* near Deepwater, W. Va. in September 1958. The long train has an RPO, express, baggage car, and many passenger-carrying cars including diner, coaches, and sleepers, and is making its way from Washington to Cincinnati. *C&O Railway photo, COHS collection.*

K-4 2-8-4 Kanawha type No. 2705 brings a coal train into Handley, W. Va. yard about 1948. The Kanawha River is seen at right. Handley was the division point where the New River and Kanawha Subdivisions joined. The powerful and versatile K-4 could be seen on coal trains, fast freights, and even passenger trains.
C&O Railway photo, COHS collection.

The Kanawha Subdivision

At the little town of Handley, only two miles west of the small city of Montgomery was the yard, engine terminal, and division point separating the New River and Kanawha Subdivisions of C&O's main line. The usual facilities were here including a large coaling station, roundhouse with attached machine shop, ready tracks, and water station, in addition to a yard with considerable capacity. This yard served not only for the main line trains operating through it from other points but was the terminal point for coal mine shifters serving the Cabin Creek and Paint Creek branches and the smaller lines off these branches. Trains of coal assembled at Handley were dispatched both east and west.

From Handley the Kanawha Subdivision continues to follow the river west two miles to the town of Pratt, where the coal-rich Paint Creek branch follows the meandering creek of that name through deep hollows punctuated with coal mines and tipples a high grade of coal for the industry of the nation and the world.

Seven miles west of Pratt, the Cabin Creek Subdivision branches off the main line and likewise hosts a maze of smaller branches with mines and tipples keeping mine shifter runs busy throughout the day. This line had its own marshalling yard with a small engine house and facilities at Cane Fork, ten miles up the branch from the junction.

The main line continues west from Cabin Creek Junction to Charleston, the West Virginia Capital city. Though most of the city is on the north side of the river, C&O is on the south side.

A large yellow-brick station was built at the end of a highway and foot bridge leading from the main business district of the city and served until the end of passenger business. Charleston developed a large chemical industry during and after World War II as well as other heavy industry including military ordinance, glass, and vehicle assembly, and was a good producer of high value traffic for the C&O.

The next large station beyond Charleston is St. Albans, about twelve miles to the west. It was the junction point for the Coal River Branch, or as it was known in this era the "Coal River District", comprising numerous coal-producing branches to the south. Coal River was a very strong coal producing region in the era of this book. As the river's name indicates it was a very early region of coal production even in the antebellum era, long before railroads were in the area. C&O's Coal River Branch was built at the turn of the 20th Century just as the coal boom was gaining momentum. The major marshalling yard and engine terminal for the district was 35 miles up the branch at Danville. As with the coal mined on Paint and Cabin Creeks, the Coal River production was shipped both eastward and westward. St. Albans itself had a coaling station and small engine house with a small yard only a few tracks wide. Most trains originated and terminated at Danville and went to or came from Handley or Russell, Ky.

At St. Albans, the C&O main line diverges from the Kanawha River and heads more westerly. Beyond St. Albans C&O generally follows the bed of the extinct prehistoric Teays River through several small towns including the glass making center of Milton. At Barboursville the Logan Branch diverges to the south. Like the Coal River district, it was composed of a main stem and many smaller branches. It was one of the largest originators of coal on the C&O. Its main terminal /engine facility/yard was near Logan and was called Peach Creek, about 65 miles up the line from the junction at Barboursville. This line was also built at the turn of the 20th Century, when C&O was at the height of its expansion. The yard at Peach Creek was a beehive of mine run activity and was the place where the last C&O steam locomotives operated, in the fall of 1956. At Barboursville C&O long maintained a shop facility whose job it was to take scrap and surplus materials and recondition, rehabilitate, and refurbish them for reuse, called the Barboursville Reclamation Plant.

Leaving Barboursville it is a scant eight miles to Huntington, C&O's mechanical headquarters and seat of its principal locomotive overhaul facility. C&O installed its principal shops here in 1872 and they have remained such right down to the present, with CSX still using the facility for heavy diesel locomotive repair. Freight and passenger car repair was also carried on here as well as all heavy locomotive repair for the entire system. In 1960 C&O's mechanical department moved from Richmond, Va. to Huntington, as did many operating offices. Huntington was at its height as C&O's mechanical and operating headquarters during the era of this book.

Seven miles west of Huntington's huge

Beaux Arts depot/office building is Kenova, where C&O's main line passed under that of the Norfolk & Western. A large two level Union Station served both railroads at this point. This was also the junction point with Baltimore & Ohio's Ohio River Division from Parkersburg, W. Va.

Just beyond Kenova the C&O main line crosses the Big Sandy River and enters Kentucky. The Kanawha Subdivision continues on to Russell, Ky., another ten miles, passing through the city of Ashland, where C&O had its largest on line passenger station. At Ashland passenger train sections were switched out or consolidated to and from Louisville and Detroit. Trains from the Big Sandy Subdivision also terminated here. The Big Sandy Branch left the main line at Catlettsburg, Ky., just after the main line crossed the Big Sandy, and ran up along that river for 129 miles, with many branches off its main stem. Much like the Coal River and Logan districts, Big Sandy was built in the early days of the 20th Century and steadily expanded as coal was exploited, and throughout the period supplied a prodigious flow of coal to C&O trains.

This view shows Handley yard looking east toward the engine facilities in May 1948. K-3 2-8-2 No. 1233 is in the foreground moving between rows of hopper cars. The cars closest are filled with cinders. C&O maintained a fleet of old cars which had outlived their revenue lives to use for carrying cinders away from locomotive terminals.
C&O Railway photo, COHS collection.

This overhead view shows Handley yard looking west and was taken from atop the coaling station in 1949. The caboose track is at the left and to the left of it is a string of camp cars parked behind a row of company buildings. Farther down is the depot/tower combined building that was replaced by a modern brick structure a few years after this photo was taken. A corner of the roundhouse is at the right. *COHS collection.*

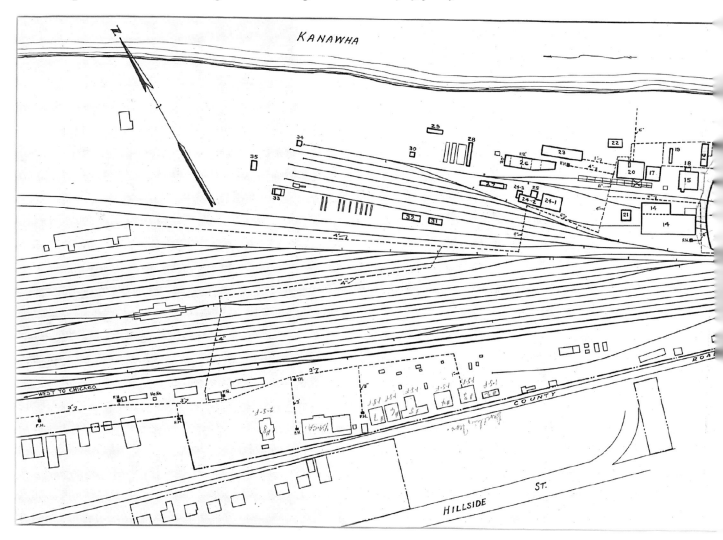

(ABOVE) This C&O Fire Prevention record map shows the structures and track layout for the Handley engine terminal and station/yard office area. *C&O Railway Drawing 9288, COHS collection.*

(BELOW) Two H-8's and a K-4 rest at the Handley engine terminal in the late 1940's. Coaling station and two water tanks were the landmarks here.

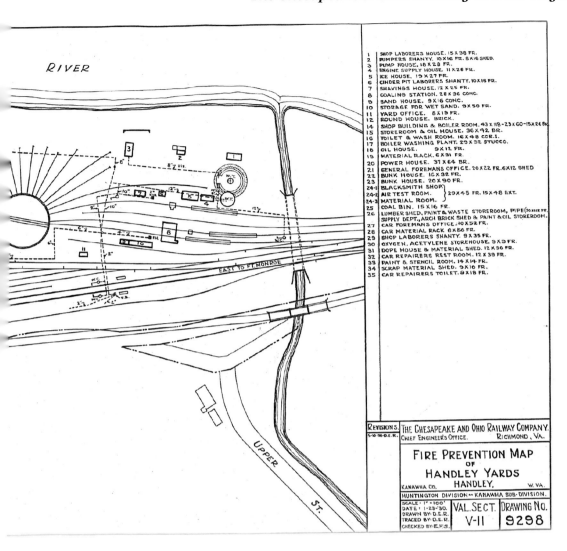

RIVER

1	SHOP LABORERS HOUSE. 15 X 38 FR.
2	PUMPERS SHANTY. 10 X 16 FR. 8 X 16 SHED.
3	PUMP HOUSE. 18 X 28 FR.
4	ENGINE SUPPLY HOUSE. 11 X 28 FR.
5	ICE HOUSE. 19 X 27 FR.
6	CINDER PIT LABORERS SHANTY. 10 X 16 FR.
7	SHAVINGS HOUSE. 12 X 25 FR.
8	COALING STATION. 28 X 36 CONC.
9	SAND HOUSE. 9 X 16 CONC.
10	STORAGE FOR WET SAND. 9 X 50 FR.
11	YARD OFFICE. 8 X 19 FR.
12	ROUND HOUSE. BRICK.
14	SHOP BUILDING & BOILER ROOM. 43 X 118 - 23 X 60 - 15 X 26 BK.
15	STOREROOM & OIL HOUSE. 36 X 92. BR.
16	TOILET & WASH ROOM. 16 X 48 COR.I.
17	BOILER WASHING PLANT. 29 X 32 STUCCO.
18	OIL HOUSE. 9 X 12 FR.
19	MATERIAL RACK. 6 X 31 FR.
20	POWER HOUSE. 37 X 64 BR.
21	GENERAL FOREMANS OFFICE. 20 X 22 FR. 6 X 12 SHED
22	BUNK HOUSE. 16 X 32 FR.
23	BUNK HOUSE. 20 X 90 FR.
24-1	BLACKSMITH SHOP.
24-2	AIR TEST ROOM. 29 X 45 FR. 15 X 48 EXT.
24-3	MATERIAL ROOM.
25	COAL BIN. 15 X 16 FR.
26	LUMBER SHED, PAINT & WASTE STOREROOM, PIPE (20 X 112 FR.)
	SUPPLY DEPT, ARCH BRICK SHED & PAINT & OIL STORERDOM.
27	CAR FOREMANS OFFICE. 40 X 56 FR.
28	CAR MATERIAL RACK 6 X 56 FR.
29	SHOP LABORERS SHANTY. 9 X 35 FR.
30	OXYGEN, ACETYLENE STOREHOUSE. 9 X 9 FR.
31	DOPE HOUSE & MATERIAL SHED. 12 X 36 FR.
32	CAR REPAIRERS REST ROOM. 12 X 39 FR.
33	PAINT & STENCIL ROOM. 14 X 14 FR.
34	SCRAP MATERIAL SHED. 9 X 10 FR.
35	CAR REPAIRERS TOILET. 8 X 18 FR.

EAST TO FT. MONROE

UPPER ST.

REVISIONS. 5-10-'38-D.E.R.

THE CHESAPEAKE AND OHIO RAILWAY COMPANY.
CHIEF ENGINEER'S OFFICE.   RICHMOND, VA.

FIRE PREVENTION MAP
OF
HANDLEY YARDS
KANAWHA CO.   HANDLEY,   W. VA.
HUNTINGTON DIVISION — KANAWHA SUB-DIVISION.

SCALE: 1"=100' DATE: 1-23-'30. DRAWN BY: D.E.R. TRACED BY: D.E.R. CHECKED BY: E.F.S.	VAL. SECT. V-11	DRAWING NO. 9298

C&O K-4 class 2-8-4 Kanawha type No. 2713 moves along just to the east of the engine terminal at Handley in 1948. *(ALL C&O Railway photos, COHS collection.)*

This 1948 scene looking westward shows Handley yard filled with a variety of cars, but mainly hoppers filled with coal that have arrived from the Cabin Creek or Paint Creek branches. 0-8-0 switcher No. 173 is making up a train. *(BOTH) C&O Railway photos, COHS collection.*

In the fall of 1955 steam is still working out of Handley, as evidenced by this H-4 class 2-6-6-2 Mallet No. 1473 moving near the roundhouse.

(LEFT) Taken the same day as the photo at the bottom of page 54, this view shows the steam-diesel transition as a Mallet's smoke drifts over a set of F7 road diesel units sitting under the coal dock. The roundhouse turntable pit is in the foreground. *(BOTH) C&O Railway photos, COHS collection.*

(BELOW) The year 1955-56 saw the last stand of steam on the C&O, and Handley was a great place to see the two competing motive power types working uneasily together. At right a K-4 has pulled a coal train into the yard, while at the left a set of four GP9s is ready to take a train out.

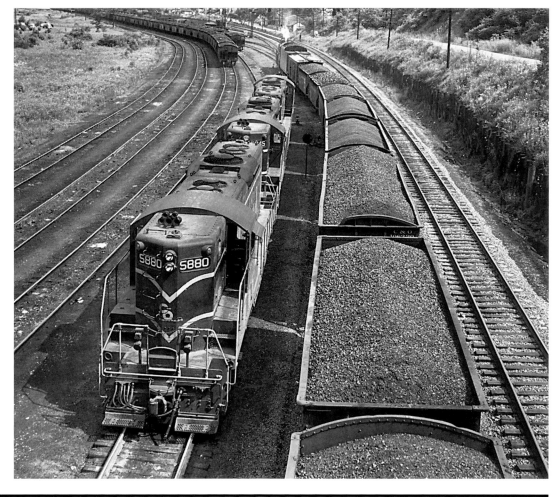

The station and tower combined building that served Handley was built in the 1890s and was once a common type structure on the C&O in W. Va. The building beside the station in the upper photo was the yard office. Modelers have long been interested in this unusual style of structure. The scene shown here in the late 1940s was soon demolished in favor of a Spartan brick yard office/tower. *(BOTH) C&O Railway photos, COHS collection.*

(ABOVE) K-4 2-8-4 Kanawha type No. 2711 powers a train west near Partt, W. Va. on the main line in May 1955. When C&O acquired 2-8-4s they didn't use the name "Berkshire" by which the type was widely known, but rather adopted "Kanawha" after the W. Va. river.

Ray Tobey, COHS collection.

(LEFT) K-3 Mikado (2-8-2) No. 1238 brings a train of loads off the Cabin Creek branch at Cabin Creek Junction. The photo was taken from the signal tower (or "Cabins" as C&O called them) in 1948 a train was made up at Cane Fork yard, about ten miles up the branch.

A.R. Hoffman, COHS collection.

(LEFT) The two-stall board-and-batten engine-house at Cane Fork was typical of many at C&O terminals where brick roundhouses weren't needed. H-4 2-6-6-2 No. 1410 rests partway in the house in 1954 being readied to take empties to mines and return with loads. *Gene Huddleston, COHS collection.*

(BELOW) Another C&O Fire Prevention map serves to show the layout of Cane Fork yard and label all the buildings. Cane Fork was located 10 miles up the Cabin Creek Subdivision and served as a marshalling point for mine runs serving the mines on the line.

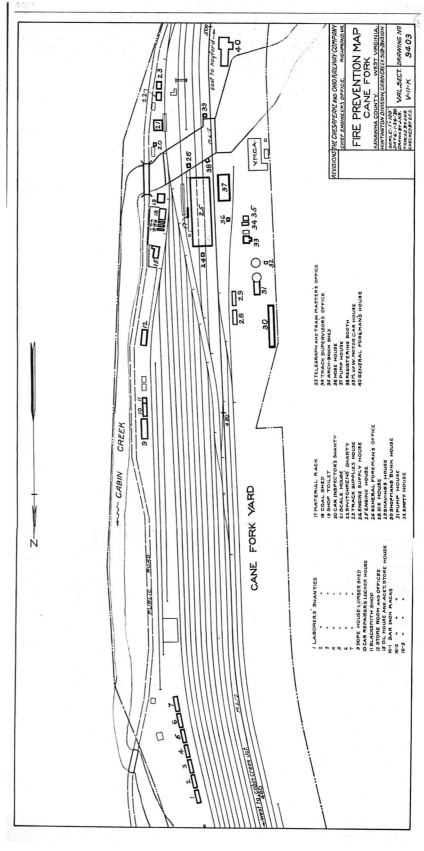

FIRE PREVENTION MAP
CANE FORK

CANE FORK YARD

1 LABORERS' SHANTIES
2 "
3 "
4 "
5 "
6 "
7 "
9 DOPE HOUSE-LUMBER SHED
10 CAR REPAIRERS LOCKER HOUSE
11 BLACKSMITH SHOP
12 STORE ROOM AND OFFICES
14 OIL HOUSE AND ACET.STORE HOUSE
16-1 BAR IRON RACKS
16-2 "
16-3 "

17 MATERIAL RACK
18 COAL SHED
19 SHOP TOILET
20 CAR INSPECTORS SHANTY
21 SCALE HOUSE
22 PUMP HOUSE
23 SWITCHMENS SHANTY
23 TRACK SUPPLIES HOUSE
24 ENGINE SUPPLY HOUSE
25 ENGINE HOUSE
26 GENERAL FOREMAN'S OFFICE
28 ICE HOUSE
29 SHAVINGS HOUSE
30 SHOPMANS BUNK HOUSE
31 PUMP HOUSE
32 EMPTY HOUSE

33 TELEGRAPH AND TRAIN MASTER'S OFFICE
34 TRACK SUPERVISOR'S OFFICE
35 ARCH-BRICK SHED
36 HOSE HOUSE
37 PUMP HOUSE
38 REGISTERING BOOTH
39 M. of W. MOTOR CAR HOUSE
40 GENERAL FOREMAN'S HOUSE

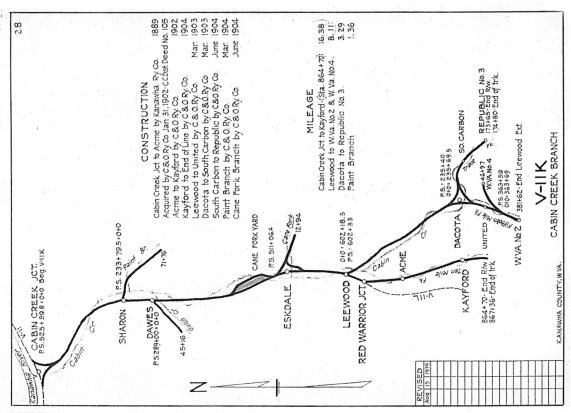

CONSTRUCTION

Cabin Creek Jct. to Acme by Kanawha Ry.Co. ... 1889
Acquired by C.&O.Ry.Co. Jan 31,1902-C.C.Dist Deed No.105
Acme to Kayford by C.&O.Ry.Co. ... 1902
Kayford to End of Line by C.&O.Ry.Co. ... 1904
Leewood to United by C.&O.Ry.Co. ... Mar. 1903
Dacota to South Carbon by C.&O.Ry.Co. ... Mar. 1903
South Carbon to Republic by C.&O.Ry.Co. ... June 1904
Paint Branch by C.&O.Ry.Co. ... Mar. 1904
Cane Fork Branch by C.&O.Ry.Co. ... June 1904

MILEAGE

Cabin Creek Jct. to Kayford:(Sta. 864+70) ... 16.38
Leewood to W.Va.No.2 & W.Va.No.4. ... 8.11
Dacota to Republic No. 3 ... 3.29
Paint Branch ... 1.36

CABIN CREEK JCT.
P.S.525+59.8+0+0 Beg. V-11K

SHARON P.S. 233+79.5+0+0

Paint Br. 71+76

DAWES P.S.289+00+0+0

45+16 Gulch

CANE FORK YARD P.S. 511+06.3

Cane Fork 12+94

ESKDALE

LEEWOOD 010+602+18.5 P.S. 602+33

RED WARRIOR JCT.

Cabin Cr.

ACME

KAYFORD 864+70+ End R/w 867+36+ End of trk.

Ten Mile Fk.

V-11L

DACOTA P.S. 235+40 010+235+69.5

SO. CARBON

Trace Cr.

Fifteen Mile Fk. 64+97 W.VA.No.4 010+363+69 P.S.363+59

UNITED

W.VA.No 2. 381+62+ End Leewood Ext.

REPUBLIC No. 3 173+65+End R/w 174+80+End of trk.

V-11K

CABIN CREEK BRANCH

KANAWHA COUNTY, W.VA.

REVISED Aug 15 1939

28

N

This Valuation Index Map shows the Cabin Creek line and gives some history about its construction. (NOTE. 8-1/2x11 size maps like this for the C&O main line and all its branches, over 120 pages, is available from the C&O Historical Society (call 800-453-COHS or go to www.chessieshop.com, look under reprints for catalog number DS-7-048 ($24.95)

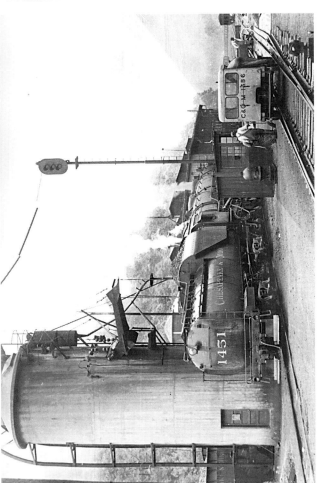

H-4 No. 1451 simmers beneath the tiny coaling station at Cane Fork terminal as track workers repair trackage around the scale house. Motor Car M- 1686 sits on the scale track. The enginehouse roof is in the background. The photo was made in June 1956, as C&O steam was gasping its last on the coal branches of West Virginia. *Gene Huddleston, COHS collection.*

A C&O H-8 2-6-6-6 with a coal train westbound rolls along the Kanawha River in Charleston, W. Va. The West Virginia capitol dome is seen in the distant background. 1949.

T. L. Wise, COHS collection

In a magnificent show of steam and exhaust C&O K-4 2-8-4 Kanawha type blasts out of Charleston station in February 1955 after a heavy snow.
A striking winter photo!

Frank Shaffer, COHS collection

Kanawha No. 2723 has an eastbound empty coal train in tow, pulling through the Charleston station in May 1955. *Ray Tobey, COHS collection.*

Located on the south side of the Kanawha River, opposite the main business district of Charleston, C&O's ca. 1906 two-story yellow brick station accommodated a large clientele as the capital city's main passenger station in the railway age. It was reached by the bridge seen at left. *C&O Railway photo, COHS collection.*

The news stand at the Charleston station faced into the waiting room and also had these display windows that fronted on the platform outside. This photo was taken in November 1947. The newsstand was removed several years later when the waiting room was renovated. The unusual station sign was used at only a few C&O locations, and also was discontinued soon after this photo. *(BOTH) C&O Railway photos, COHS collection.*

This early 1960s photo is looking west from the east end of the platform shed at the Charleston station. The baggage trucks were used for loading and unloading mail and express. It appears that one is stacked high with mail bags, probably for loading on the next train.

(RIGHT) St. Albans is the first large station west of Charleston and was the point at which the Coal River Subdivision joined the main line. The small engine terminal and coaling station here were always busy. G-9 1044 and H-6 1514 are here on this day in 1948.

(LEFT) K-4 No. 2755 takes on water at Sproul, W. Va. a junction point 15 miles up the Coal River line. Although not often thought of, water was as important as coal during the steam era, and the C&O, as most railroads, spent a great deal of money and effort to supply its locomotives with good quality water.

(ALL) C&O Railway photos, COHS collection.

(BOTTOM) The main terminal and marshalling yard for the Coal River District was at Danville, W. Va., 35 miles up the branch from St. Albans. Trains were assembled here which went east to Handley and west to Russell. This overhead view was taken in June 1950.

(LEFT) Along the straight and well maintained double-track C&O main line near Culloden, W. Va. a K-4 Kanawha moves a fast freight eastward at a high speed. Just as H-8s were the most common steam power on the Alleghany Subdivision in the 1940s and early 1950s, the K-4s were on the Kanawha Subdivision.

(ALL) C&O Railway photos, COHS collection.

(RIGHT) Although C&O was known for its Cantilever signal bridges, the main line also had many full bridges such as this one at Barboursville, W. Va. under which K-4 2736 brings a manifest freight in 1946.

From Barboursville the Logan Subdivision branched to the south and encompassed a maze of branches serving scores of mines. Coal was marshalled at Peach Creek Yard in Logan, 64 miles south of the main line. Here many steam locomotives await assignments.

(LEFT) H-6 2-6-6-2 No. 1307 makes a wonderful show of white exhaust near Logan in 1955 during the last winter of steam on the C&O. The last order for 10 H-6s, was delivered in 1948 even though the design was an exact replica of the earlier H-6s, built in the 1920s! It's ironic that No. 1308, which was the very last steam locomotive built commercially for any railroad in the United States, and it was from a 40-year old design. It was on September 26, 1956 that H-4 No. 1475 made a mine shifter run out of Peach Creek, its return run was never dispatched again. In fact no other steam locomotive was dispatched on the C&O and the steam age ended at that time.

C&O Railway photo, COHS collection.

(BELOW) This reduced map shows the Logan Subdivision. To understand how the many branches tied in look at the map on page 16.

K-4 No. 2731 is moving eastbound with a manifest freight train across the Guyandotte River bridge on the eastern outskirts of Huntington, W. Va. November 1951. *Gene Huddleston, COHS collection.*

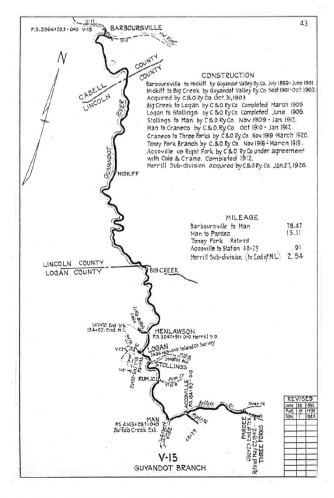

The steam-diesel transition is evident at Huntington yard as new Alco RSD-5 No. 5587 meets K4 2-8-4 2707 in June 1953.

Gene Huddleston, COHS collection.

Another of the ubiquitous K-4s, No. 2778, is passing the Huntington depot with westbound freight in 1955.

No. 4012 one of C&O's brand new E8 passenger diesels is seen here on a westbound train at Huntington just arriving. After consolidation of mainline trains resulting in longer consists, the coupler cowl was removed and a multiple-unit plug was placed in the nose of these units so that they could be operated in sets of three instead of the two seen here.

(BOTH) C&O Railway photo, COHS collection.

(LEFT) An ABA set of FP7s, with No. 8002 leading rolls a manifest freight train through Huntington yards in the winter of 1956. In addition to its stable of F7 units, C&O also bought several sets of FP7s. The "P" indicates that it is equipped with a steam generator for use on passenger trains. The B units that were used with these sets were straight F7B's, but all the units were painted in the passenger scheme instead of the freight paint scheme. They were used for extra work, excursions, standby, and on branch trains such as the Big Sandy local, but most often they were in freight service as seen here.

(BELOW) When diesels arrived C&O built new enginehouses for them at Huntington, W. Va., Clifton Forge, Va., and Peru, Indiana a modernistic design such as the Huntington building seen here. Note the switchers and an E8 on the service tracks. Taken just after the new facility opened in 1955.

(BOTH) C&O Railway photo, COHS collection.

This aerial view shows the huge Huntington, W. Va. C&O shop facilities. From the 1870s forward C&O did all it's major locomotive repair and maintenance at Huntington. In the early 1950s the shop was converted to diesel maintenance in a highly publicized program where the employees were allowed to design the new facility themselves. This 1956 view shows the complex at the peak of its activity. The basic shop buildings are still used as a major repair facility for CSX Transportation, C&O's successor. *C&O Railway photo, COHS collection.*

This marvelous photo shows the erecting bay of the Huntington shops filled with steam locomotives in various states of disassembly for major repairs. Note the boiler flues out of the Mikado closest.

(BOTH) C&O Railway photos, COHS collection.

Two Huntington shop employees apply an eccentric rod to the running gear of a C&O F-19 Pacific type locomotive in 1943. Although some general repair work was done at outlying shops, all heavy rebuilds and major repair for all C&O steam was done at Huntington. Clifton Forge, Va. shops could do some of this if the Huntington work load was too great.

(ABOVE) Nothing is more dramatic in a steam locomotive shop than "wheeling" an engine. Here at the Huntington Shops erecting bay in mid-1940s, 2-8-2 No. 1169 is being lowered onto drivers and leading truck wheels as employees look on and guide the crane operator.

(ALL) C&O Railway photos, COHS collection.

(ABOVE) Huntington shop employees gauge the axle of a set of driving wheels with roller bearings in 1943.

(RIGHT) One of the impressive functions of the Huntington machine shop was to machine driving wheels on a large lathe. Two employees are working on one set of wheels while others await attention.

Although the erecting bay at Huntington in the diesel era looks about as impressive as it did during the steam age, the maintenance work on diesels was easier and they operated better and at longer stretches between maintenance. Parts were standardized, and fewer employees were needed for heavy maintenance. A wide variety of first-generation diesels is seen in this 1961 photo.
C&O Railway photos, COHS collection.

The C&O main line leaving Huntington passed through a town known as Kenova, so named because it was at the junction point of Kentucky, Ohio, and West Virginia. Here K-4 No. 2724 has a westbound coal train in tow, passing strings of wooden camp cars in September 1955.

Ray Tobey, COHS collection.

In a classic scene K-4 No. 2731, the usual power for Kanawha Subdivision trains in the late 1940s to the end of steam, powers a westbound coal train with a magnificent show of exhaust, in May 1955. Though a time honored scene it would be repeated fewer and fewer times until about 18 months after this photo was taken it would be no more. *Ray Tobey, COHS collection.*

In September 1947, classically proportioned C&O F-15 Pacific type (4-6-2) No. 440 is stopped at the two-level Kenova Union Station, serving N&W's Cincinnati-Norfolk trains on the top level. This train, local train No. 7, has a mail and express car, a full express car and two coaches, it is making its trip between Hinton and Cincinnati covering all the small stations. *Gene Huddleston, COHS collection.*

K-4 No. 2747 crosses the Big Sandy River bridge with a heavy manifest freight train (note the refrigerator cars up front) in about 1948. The Big Sandy formed the border between West Virginia and Kentucky at this point. The C&O main line left the West Virginia bank, crossed over into Kentucky and reached the city of Ashland. There it maintained the largest passenger station on the line.   At Russell, C&O's huge yard, became the largest railroad facility owned by a single line in the world in the mid-1950s. It was at Russell that the Kanawha Subdivision actually ended. The Big Sandy bridge prevented the movement of certain C&O steam locomotives, namely the T-1, to the West Virginia side until it was rebuilt and strengthened in the late 1940s. It was at that time that the 2-10-4s were occasionally allowed east of Russell. With the crossing of the Big Sandy the C&O main line has traveled 203 miles from Tuckahoe, in a generally west-northwest direction to the Big Sandy crossing. The total mileage of the C&O in West Virginia in 1948 was 1,511.1 miles when all the coal branches are included, more than in any of the other seven states and one Canadian province that it served. *C&O Railway photo, COHS collection.*

Color Album

Blackened with heavy usage in tunnels, a C&O GP9 and three others with an empty hopper train at Tuckahoe, W.Va. just out of Alleghany Tunnel. Tuckahoe was the first station on the West Virginia side of the tunnel which straddled the state line. July 1960. *Photo by Gene Huddleston.*

At Tuckahoe, the long curve offered ample opportunity for the photographer. Here we see E8 4018 with train No. 5/47, the westbound *Sportsman*, passing an eastbound work train with a red C&O caboose. The *Sportsman* would make it's next stop at White Sulphur Springs, about 5 miles from this spot. July 1960. *Photo by Gene Huddleston.*

This is an eastbound coal train on the long curve at Tuckahoe, again powered by five GP9s, led by No. 6246, undoubtedly working very hard with their loaded train almost to the tunnel at the summit of the eastbound grade. *Photo by Gene Huddleston.*

Five GP9s, led by 6253, emerge from White Sulphur Tunnel with manifest freight train No. 95 in June of 1960. The bright yellow of a refrigerator car is seen just out of the murk of the tunnel. *Photo by Gene Huddleston.*

(TOP LEFT) This beautiful overhead photo shows the unusual layout of Ft. Spring, W.Va. with it's modern station situated in the short space between two tunnels. The train has emerged from Mann's Tunnel in the distance and is about to enter the new Ft. Spring Tunnel below the photographer. (TOP RIGHT) An eastbound coal train powered by GP9s is about to enter the west portal of Big Bend Tunnel at Hilldale, W.Va. (MW Cabin signal tower is seen in the background). April 1961. (BELOW) This view shows the NF&G engine terminal area at Rainelle, W.Va. Numerous C&O GP9s are just in front of the engine house and a string of cabooses (several red and one yellow) sit at right. All waiting for use on mine runs. June 1960. *Photos by Gene Huddleston*

In June 1960, a C&O train is nearly obscured in brake smoke as it descends the NF&G loops near Claypool, W.Va, en route from Rainelle yard to Meadow Creek on the main line. The loops replaced switch-backs on this very steep portion of the line in the late 1940's. *Photo by Gene Huddleston*

(ABOVE) A train with lumber loads has just come down from Rainelle and is about to enter the C&O main line Meadow Creek. MD Cabin signal tower is in the background. *Photo by Gene Huddleston*
(BELOW) Coming from the Winding Gulf Subdivision and headed for Raleigh, W.Va. Yard, a C&O mine shifter emerges from tunnel at Tunnel Siding late in the afternoon in July 1958. The brakeman is wearing traditional gauntlet gloves. *Photo by Gene Huddleston*

(ABOVE) A brace of five C&O GP9's lead by No. 5985 has an empty coal train on the New River Subdivision main line at Eagle, W.Va. The smoke in the background was from the Electro-Metallurgical plant (now Elkem Metals) at Alloy. June 1962.
Photo by Gene Huddleston
(BELOW) The Paint Creek shifter backs up the branch at Imperial Junction. Two GP9's led by No. 6136 are in charge this day in June 1962. *Photo by Gene Huddleston*

(ABOVE) This December 1960 snow scene depicts the C&O's engine terminal area in the Danville, W.Va. coal marshalling yard. Road locomotives are getting ready to take a coal train to Russell or Handley. *Photo by Gene Huddleston*
(BELOW) A mine shifter out of Danville near West Junction in December 1960 has GP9 No. 6011 at the head in a heavy snow storm. The Coal River District always produced a large quantity of coal for the C&O and still does for CSXT. *Photo by Gene Huddleston*

(TOP LEFT) This interesting scene looking west was taken near the Huntington shops in December 1964. At left, GP9's have manifest freight No. 92 and F7's can been seen in the distance picking up from 16th Street Yard, while a switcher with cars for the Barboursville Reclamation Plant is ready to leave behind No. 92. *Photo by Gene Huddleston*

(TOP RIGHT) A long string of beautiful C&O passenger cars comprise train No. 3 - *The Fast Flying Virginian*, as it swings around the curve just east of the Huntington shops. November 1963. *Photo by Gene Huddleston*

(LEFT) GP9 No. 6093 rests below the recently retired coaling tower at Cane Fork Yard in 1962. Although steam had been gone for more than six years, the coaling station still looks to be in good condition. Cane Fork was the major collecting yard for coal runs on the Cabin Creek Branch, from which they were sent down the branch to Handley. *Photo by Gene Huddleston*

(ABOVE) On the Logan Subdivision near Chapmanville, F7 No. 7003 in its original paint and a second F7A in the "simplified paint scheme" bring a coal train down the Guyandotte River toward Barboursville where the train will gain the mainline and travel west to Russell, KY Yard. A cold day in December, 1960. Photo by Gene Huddleston

(BELOW) FP7 No. 8007 and F7 power and eastbound freight across the Mud River Bridge near Barboursville, W.Va., in the fall of 1962. The C&O purchased 14 FP7As and two B-Units in early 1952, using them to dieselize the last of it's passenger operations and as standby units for special movements, etc. When they weren't in passenger service, they were used on freights. By the time this photo was taken, passenger service had declined and there were enough E8's to handle all the trains, so the FP7's were given regular freight assignments. They wore the three-color paint scheme of the E8's and were numbered in the series 8000-8013.

Resources

Listed below are some books and publications that deal with C&O History in general, and others that bear more particularly on the C&O in West Virginia. Some are in print and available from the C&O Historical Society at the time of printing this book, and others are out of print and would have to be consulted through libraries or purchased secondhand.

General C&O History

Chessie's Road - Revised edition, 1993, by Charles Turner, updated by Eugene L. Huddleston & Thomas W. Dixon, Jr. - Hardbound, 324 pages, fully illustrated, C&O Hist. Soc. Imprint. (*)

Chesapeake & Ohio For Progress, the C&O at Mid-20th Century, Edited by Thomas W. Dixon, Jr., and Kevin Holland, Hardbound 144 pages (Expected to be issued in late-2005) (*)

Publications Focused on C&O in W. Va.

Chesapeake & Ohio's Alleghany Subdivision, by Thomas W. Dixon, Jr., 1985, Softbound, 128 pages, fully illus., C&O Hist. Soc. Imprint. (out of print)

Riding That New River Train, by Eugene L. Huddleston, 128 pages, Softbound, 1989, 1993, C&O Hist. Soc. Imprint (out of print)

The Chesapeake & Ohio in West Virginia - Huntington Division, by William R. Sparkmon, Softbound, 64 pages, 1983, Jalamap Pub. Imprint (out of print)

Chesapeake & Ohio in the Coal Fields, by Thomas W. Dixon, Jr., Hardbound, 112 pages, fully illustrated, 1995, C&O Hist. Soc. Imprint (out of print).

Chesapeake & Ohio in West Virginia - Mainlines and Mine Runs, by Thomas W. Dixon, Jr., Softbound, 64 pages, Carstens Publications, 1985 (out of print).

Chesapeake & Ohio in Thurmond, W. Va., 2004, Softbound, 48 pgs, C&O Hist. Soc. Imprint (*)

Chesapeake & Ohio in Thurmond, W. Va. - CD ROM, C&O Hist. Society Compact Disc with above booklet plus scores of additional photos and drawings giving the complete Thurmond picture, fully serachable and printable. (*)

Thurmond, A New River Community, Softbound, 46 pages Eastern National Imprint (Nat. Park Service), illus. (*)

Kaymoor, 54 pages, Softbound, Eastern National Imprint (National Park Service) (*)

Sewell, by Ron Lane, 46 pages, Softbound, Eastern National Imprint (Nat. Park Service) (*)

Chesapeake & Ohio Coal & Color, by Engine L. Huddleston, John Joseph & Everett Young,1997, C&O Hist. Soc. Imprint, 128 pages, fully illus. in color. (*)

Chesapeake & Ohio in Color, Vol. 2 - William Mc Clure and Jeremy Plant, 128 pages, full color illustrations, Morning Sun Books Imprint (*)

(*) - Available (2005) from C&O Historical Society (800-453-COHS or www.chessieshop.com)